STRESS RELIEF & RELAXATION TECHNIQUES

ALSO BY JUDITH LAZARUS:
The Spa Sourcebook

Stress Relief & Relaxation Techniques

JUDITH LAZARUS

KEATS PUBLISHING

LOS ANGELES

NTC/Contemporary Publishing Group

Library of Congress Cataloging-in-Publication Data

Lazarus, Judith.
    Stress relief & relaxation techniques / Judith Lazarus.
        p. cm.
    Includes bibliographical references and index.
    ISBN 0-658-00385-2
        1. Stress (Psychology) 2. Stress management. I. Title: Stress relief
    and relaxation techniques. II. Title.

    BF575.S75 L294 2000
    155.9'042–dc21
                                                                00-028697

Published by Keats Publishing.
A division of NTC/Contemporary Publishing Group, Inc.
4255 West Touhy Avenue, Lincolnwood, Illinois 60646-1975 U.S.A.

Copyright © 2000 by Judith Lazarus.

Design by Laurie Young

Printed in the United States of America

International Standard Book Number: 0-658-00385-2

00 01 02 03 04 VP 18 17 16 15 14 13 12 11 10 9 8 7 6 5 4 3 2 1

For Jerry, Maureen, Jason, Matthew, Ron, Rob, Heidi, Aaron, Max, Alexandra, Da-Da, Suki, and the three generations of eternally barking dogs next door, my husband, children, children-in-law, grandchildren, brother and sister, who are my most persistent stressors and—except for the dogs—my greatest sources of endorphins.

CONTENTS

2

3

Contents

ACKNOWLEDGMENTS

First and always, thanks go to my husband, Jerry, whose life partnership I treasure. Though we are always each other's cheerleaders, he went above and beyond to help me get through this project. We have always taken turns giving and receiving stress, but during the time I wrote the book, he took more than he gave.

I am ever grateful for my children and grandchildren, who inspire me to achieve things that they can be proud of and who make everything worthwhile.

For being supportive and encouraging, my friends deserve thanks, especially those who are my mentors as well: Rena Copperman and Martha McCarty Weiler, I couldn't have done it without you.

Thank you to my editor, Peter Hoffman, and my copy editor, Steve Baeck, for helping me to make a book out of mountains of research.

I appreciate the time the experts spent on the phone and Internet with me, with special thanks to Drs. Herbert Benson, Stan Charnofsky, Deepak Chopra, Raymond Flannery Jr., Carl Hammerschlag, Joyce C. Mills, Pamela Peeke, David Rapkin, Andrew Weil, Jon Kabat-Zinn, and William B. Malarkey.

Most of all, I want to acknowledge the important contributions of stress-management therapists, researchers, professionals, and gurus everywhere who are helping us to create a new paradigm of wellness. I believe that if we can learn to better manage our stressors and to be good to ourselves, we can be kinder and more understanding of others. Then, we can make a better world.

INTRODUCTION

STRESS MANAGEMENT:
WHO NEEDS IT?

How many times have you said to yourself, "How will I ever get
through this day?" Hundreds, I'll bet. People are tested and
stretched almost beyond their limits by factors obvious and inex-
plicable all the time. I don't know where the description *normal*
comes from, because no one I know has a "normal" life.

One night, I almost didn't make it to a dinner party at
which a friend and I began ruminating about stress management
and who could benefit from it. He has a successful business that
he manages quite well, a wife he adores, and two lovely daugh-
ters. Still, he told me he goes ballistic if the TV cable goes out—
his veins pop out, his heart beats fast, his stomach churns, he goes
into a rage. Where does an extreme reaction to an everyday

inconvenience come from? As it turns out, every member of his family had recently experienced a health or emotional crisis.

What almost kept me away that night was that my book deadline was only four weeks away, and I was behind schedule. I didn't have time to keep up with the E-mail, junk mail, and snail mail, let alone wait for repairmen: Our TV had broken, the toilet wouldn't stop running, and the air conditioner was on the fritz. Of course, they couldn't make it all on the same day, so I was trying to stay alert for the doorbell for the "somewhere between 8 A.M. and 5 P.M." visits while trying to concentrate on my work from my office in the back of the house. The next-door neighbors had gone off on vacation, leaving three big dogs to bark from morning until night just under the window of my office.

My car had been erratically stalling, but it was running fine when I drove it to the mechanic, who told me he couldn't tell what was wrong if it wasn't malfunctioning at that moment. I had to prepare for a business trip in the middle of all this, and was trying to do laundry, cancel the paper and mail delivery, notify delivery services, and—hardest of all—decide what to wear. We won't even talk about the bills, the groceries, the cleaning, the cooking. Exercise? Fuggedaboutit.

My husband hadn't been feeling well for a few weeks, so we had to go to the hospital for tests. That was the eve of our daughter's planned camping trip with four other families. Our almost-one-year-old grandson came down with a case of croup. When they returned home, after being caught in a sudden, torrential rainstorm that forced them off the road for hours, we found out a friend's mother who had been holding our grandson all weekend had come down with the chicken pox—one week before his birthday party. Our four-year-old grandson developed an ear infection. Our three other children had minor crises that week, too, as did my bachelor brother and newly divorced sister. Two friends were in the hospital with serious illnesses, and a cousin died. All these problems required hours of venting, discussing, and problem solving on the phone.

Days were spent attending to these unplanned emergencies, so I was at my computer until four or five each morning in order to keep up. And I had health problems of my own: I was recovering from a back injury and fighting a low-grade fever.

Back to the party: Everyone was talking about the problems in their lives. Everyone was trying to cope. Ill health, wayward teens, problems at work, money troubles, difficult bosses . . . *this* was what was "normal."

So who needs stress management? We all do. Stressors happen—we can't avoid them, but how we handle them makes all the difference to our health and happiness. Some call it the "Rubber Band Theory." When you stretch an elastic band almost to its limits, then let it relax into its original shape, you can use and reuse it many times. If you pull it taut beyond its limits, it will break. Everything has a breaking point.

Great news, though: Medical science has discovered that relaxation and stress-management techniques actually counter the effects of these stressors. They can relax the rubber band of tension: lower blood pressure, clear muddled thinking, reduce anxiety, slow heartbeat, regulate breathing and oxygen intake, and stimulate the hormones that allow the body to calm and heal itself.

Of course, there are some life circumstances and tragedies that are harder to deal with than others. Still, we don't usually have the choice of whether we want to face major crises or not: They just happen. We can help ourselves get through the worst in the best way, and make the merely bad-hair days a lot easier.

For as long as I can remember, I've suffered from floating anxiety. Even before I became a real Jewish mother I worried about everything, mostly things way beyond my control. When I had the opportunity to start learning about relaxation therapies while researching a book about spas, a whole new world opened to me. The problems didn't go away, but *I* learned how to go away—at least long enough to recharge.

Why did I write this book? I've been writing about health and lifestyle for many years, and I've noticed that there seems to be a tidal wave of yearning for self-knowledge and spirituality, which I suspect is a backlash against our mainstream preoccupation with high technology. History shows, though, that this desire for mastering ourselves and connecting with the universe is by no means new, even if it seemed to go underground for a while. Many of the techniques that science is saying are "new" have been around for thousands of years.

A common thread runs through this book. It doesn't seem to matter who we are, or where we come from; what our religion, color, race, or profession is; we need to get back to a sense of our true selves. We have to find a way to meet our responsibilities and yet maintain a sense of humanity and wholeness, find joy and peace in our lives, connect with our higher selves and to a Greater Power. Even if you believe this is all there is, that it has nothing to do with a karmic path or the road to glory, you want to make the best of this life. The last of the baby boomers will be reaching what used to be retirement age any year now, and we are living longer. If you want to live better, today and tomorrow, a balanced life will serve you well.

By the time you've finished this book, you'll see how the philosophies and techniques of stress management connect and enhance each other. When you find ones that "speak to you," go out and expand your knowledge. There are books, videos, audiotapes, CDs, Web sites, and television and radio shows offering a bounty of relaxation and self-awareness practices.

You will be amazed at how little time it takes to help yourself become more resilient, more able to redeem happiness and health. Stress experts agree with one another about the basic requirements of that pursuit. When you are resistant to the ravages of stress, you can explore your higher self for a deeper sense of meaning and a feeling of belonging to the universal family. Read on and you're sure to find an approach that's right for you.

Stress Relief
& Relaxation
Techniques

What Is Stress?

I saw a woman in the aisle of a grocery store pushing a cart, which held a screaming toddler. In a very calm, quiet voice she was saying, "Don't scream, Jessica. Don't yell, Jessica. Be calm." I had to admire the way she handled the stress of that moment. I went over to her and told her how wonderfully I thought she dealt with her baby. She replied, "I am Jessica."

—RABBI BERNARD COHEN

Stress. Just reading the word can make your stomach roil, your jaw clench, your shoulders tighten. The word carries a lot of baggage, reminding you of all your problems and the woes of the world. For some, stress comes with a built-in catch-22: Just the thought that they must *do* something about stress can make them feel ineffectual, powerless, and even more anxious. The key thing to remember for stress management—or rather, distress management—is that stress is not a *thing*; it's a reaction to things. There is a whole world of tools and techniques that can help you react in ways that are productive rather than destructive.

Stress isn't all bad. "Without stress, there would be no life," says Paul J. Rosch, M.D., president of the American Institute of Stress and clinical professor of medicine and psychiatry at New

1

York Medical College. "However, just as distress can cause disease, there are good stresses that offset this, and promote wellness." Balancing the good and bad is no easy trick. "It's very much like the stress on a violin string," according to Rosch. "Not enough produces a dull, raspy sound. Too much makes a shrill, annoying noise, or causes the string to snap. However, just the right degree can produce magnificent tones." The techniques and practices in this book might help you make your own beautiful music.

One can't avoid all the things that contribute to stress, but one can learn new approaches to counterbalance their effects. The National Institutes of Health (NIH) has established an Office of Alternative Medicine to find out which techniques and practices live up to their Eastern, Oriental, Indian, European, and Native American folkloric reputations for holistic healing. On its Web site, the NIH defines *holistic* as describing "therapies based on facts about the 'whole person,' including spiritual and mental aspects, not only the specific part of the body being treated. Holistic practitioners may advise changes in diet, physical activity, and other lifestyle factors to help relieve a patient's condition."

To help ease conditions aggravated by stress, a relaxation response can be mastered that will counteract the natural tendency toward "fight or flight," according to noted researcher and author Herbert Benson, M.D., founding president of the Mind/Body Medical Institute at the Beth Israel Deaconess Medical Center in Boston. Relaxation techniques can be used to lower one's own blood pressure and repair some of the body's self-protective elements. Benson says, "Stress comes from any situation or circumstance that requires behavioral adjustment. Any change, either good or bad, is stressful, and whether it's a positive or negative change, the physiological response is the same."

Although some stress is positive (after all, no one grows from a comfort zone, and deadlines often push us into doing some good work), negative stress can take an enormous toll on one's body and mind. Studies have demonstrated its powerful influence on physical and mental health. "Science has now shown that chronic, unrelenting stress causes a gradual breakdown of every body system," says Pamela Peeke, M.D., M.P.H., who was the first senior research fellow in the National Institutes of Health's Office of Alternative Medicine.

"This toxic response needs to be neutralized to extend the quality and length of life," she adds. Author of *Fight Fat After Forty* and a noted clinical scientist studying stress physiology, Peeke says it is actually simple to control this. "Every day, take time to get away from the craziness," she advises. "Walk away from it, talk about it with loved ones, and even more important than all, simply learn to handle it better."

There really are simple techniques that allow you to be your own healer. In the past, stress complaints were trivialized with advice such as "It's all in your mind, so just change your mind," "See a psychiatrist and get some medication," or "Time heals all wounds" and "Just get over it." Sometimes, however, that advice has great value.

Your grandmother was onto something when she suggested you "take a deep breath and count to ten" or "sit down and have a cup of tea." Breathing techniques and thinking things through after the heat of the moment go a long way toward cutting bad stress off at the pass. But perhaps Grandma in her heyday didn't

3

have an answering machine on her phone, a fax, stacks of E-mail, a cell phone, a pager, or a life in which one is expected to be completely accessible "24-7." Although the way you react to stress has a lot to do with your mind, it is inextricably linked with your body and spirit and can therefore manifest in physical illness and counterproductive emotional reactions.

Peeke says, "It's only toxic and stressful if you believe it is. Remind yourself that self-destruction under stress helps no one. Self-destruction destroys immune function and foreshortens your life."

There are easy things one can do to help reclaim one's serenity. "It can be done through meditation, hatha yoga, or diaphragmatic breathing," says David Rapkin, Ph.D., director of the Mind–Body Medicine Group in the Division of Head and Neck Surgery at UCLA. "And it's easily taught," he adds. "Breathing is the single most important thing that sets our interior climate or atmosphere. It increases our mental staying power, sharpness, and skill."

"The stresses in our lives are not events," says Carl A. Hammerschlag, M.D., a Yale-trained psychiatrist, author of *The Dancing Healers*, and lecturer. He has worked with Native American cultures and recognizes the wisdom in their approaches to wellness. "How you come to the stressful events in your life is more important than the events themselves."

Hammerschlag uses psychoneuroimmunology (PNI) to address how the combination of our life experiences, of both mind and body, affects our reactions to stress and illness. PNI is the study of how our bodies and minds interact to affect our well-being. "It is a simple technique for attitude adjustment," he says. "The most critical adjustment people need to make in dealing with stress is to reprogram their thinking to understand that stress is not an event, but their reaction to it. Once you recognize that that is not what does you in, but the choices you make in dealing with it, you can regain control of your destiny."

The awareness that you have a choice to act on or react to a stressful event allows you to face the inevitable stressors head-on. "You can't let the events of your life define your participating. The greatest power is the power of choice," Hammerschlag says.

Can We Talk?

Language affects our thoughts, behaviors, and actions. Neurolinguistic programming, an alternative psychotherapy technique, can help you assess whether you are using language to help or hurt yourself, and to help you find new ways of communicating with yourself and others for positive effect. Next time you're stressed out, ask yourself

- What exactly is the problem?
- Why is it happening?
- How does it make you feel?
- What does it stop you from doing that you want to do?
- What does it make you do that you do not want to do?
- Does this happen often?
- What can you do to change your stressful reaction if it happens again?

5

Try to become aware of your reactions, and reframe your thoughts from negative to positive, or at least neutral. Do you see a difference in "I just can't do this alone!" and "I can definitely ask for help"? Your body can tell the difference, and this is one of the principles of neurolinguistic programming.

CAN YOU MAKE IT ALL GO AWAY?

We all face daily personal crises. We can't control weather, traffic, the moods of others. We can't foresee emergency trips to the vet, or the new strain of influenza that's knocking out everyone at work. Add politics, war, famine, taxes, and pollution into the mix and it's a miracle we can cope at all. Even on days when things seem to be going well, the morning paper features stress-inducing headlines about hate crimes, natural disasters, and terrible accidents. Murder and mayhem don't set the stage for a peaceful and serene outlook. Television offers the same awful news, often throwing in a teaser: "Today, on the five o'clock news: how to manage your stress in two minutes." It turns out, however, that you have to suffer through twenty minutes of tragedy to hear the stress-management tip they're offering, adding even more stress to your day.

Canadian physiologist Hans Selye, M.D., Ph.D., D.Sc., the father of modern stress theory, defined stress as "the nonspecific response of the body to any demand made upon it." In 1936 he wrote the first scientific paper defining stress and showed that stress can be a good thing when it provides us with a challenge. Problems arise only when the challenges become excessive or chronic and the body cannot cope.

6

Selye's theory, called General Adaptation Syndrome, claims that your body has the ability to maintain a healthy equilibrium in the face of a stressor. But if the stress continues unabated, your system shuts down. This inability to bounce back can lead to adrenal exhaustion and leaves the immune system vulnerable to distress and disease.

Selye continued his work on stress with hundreds of scientific papers and thirty-nine books. His work continues through Selye-Toffler University, a private graduate studies institution founded with futurist Alvin Toffler, which addresses what it calls "society's three most challenging issues: Stress, Change, and the Future," in an on-line learning environment.

The prevailing wisdom is that even a few minutes of relaxation can combat the stressors, although twenty minutes or more is recommended. The aforementioned Dr. Benson says that the relaxation response is "an inborn set of physiological changes that offset those of the fight-or-flight syndrome." In his continuing studies, he determined that regularly invoking the relaxation response, together with a feeling of spirituality, could be a natural defense against the effects of daily stressors. He identified what he coined "The Faith Factor."

Have faith that the stress in your life can be managed. If you're reading this book, chances are you want to learn how but may not be convinced that you can do it, if you have time for it, or if you really need it at all. The amazing thing is you don't have to worry if you're doing it right, or practice only a specific technique. If you want to relax, you can just do it.

Deepak Chopra, M.D., chairman and cofounder of The Chopra Center for Well Being in La Jolla, California, and author of twenty-five books on stress, spirituality, and human potential, says, "Stress management is the first thing you need to do to manage your life. Then you can move on to a deeper realm of experience and explore your spiritual potential."

Meditation studies can help you examine your responses to stress, and help you be more creative and intuitive in dealing with them. Anyone can do it, but Chopra says, "For these practices to work, you have to be open to them, and to make them a priority in life."

Despite a nonstop (and worldwide) itinerary, Chopra maintains the stamina to explore the universe by practicing what he preaches. He meditates each morning from 4 to 6 A.M.; takes a thirty-minute meditation break later in the day; makes time to write for at least one hour; and does a mental process before sleep, a mystical meditation incorporating mythology.

"People who say they have no time seem to find time for TV, tabloids, and gossiping on the phone," he observes. Nonetheless, he does not believe you should cajole, manipulate, seduce, or beg anyone to do anything. "When people are ready, they will find what is appropriate for them."

CAUSES OF STRESS

Stress is what happens when our normal balance is upset. When wild animals threatened the cavemen, a hormone called adrenaline would be released into their systems to activate defense mechanisms for survival. Adrenaline, or epinephrine, is a stress hormone that causes one's heart to pound, blood pressure to rise, breathing to quicken, eyes to dilate, senses to heighten, muscles to tense—all preparing the body to resist or retreat. This is commonly known as the "fight-or-flight response." It takes the body's functions away from their normal tasks, and marshals them to survival mode. When a stress reaction occurs, adrenaline and other body chemicals such as cortisol and ACTH flood one's system. Unfortunately, the hormones the body produces when we need hyperawareness for survival can become toxic when they're not required.

Although our well-being is no longer threatened by wild animals on the same large scale, that near wreck on the freeway or your child's newly pierced tongue may cause your body to react as cavemen did to wildlife. Today, the things we "fight" are more symbolic, less likely to be attacking our physical safety, says Benson. They are more apt to be threats to our pride, security, and self-esteem, or to be reviving old emotional hurts. The negative effects take their toll: Accelerated heartbeat stresses the arteries; excess glucose stays in the bloodstream instead of being metabolized immediately; the fats may stick as plaque inside blood vessels, possibly leading to heart attack or stroke.

Life events are stressful, and even good ones upset the balance. A healthy marriage, a planned pregnancy, a new job, or a brand-new house can fluster us as much as an unforeseen illness, death, or divorce. And stress can live on long after the stressor first shows up.

External stressors run the gamut from noise and air pollution, bright light, extremes of temperature, and crowds to problems with family, money, work, neighbors, red tape, or traffic. Internal stressors such as loneliness and emotional conflict are constant challenges. And certain personality traits do not lend

9

themselves to stress-free living. Are you hyperself-critical, pessimistic, or a worrywart? Do you tend to take everything personally, or think in black-and-white terms? You probably have persistent internal stress. Are you a people-pleaser or a workaholic? If so, you will greatly benefit from relaxation practices.

Unhealthy lifestyle choices can be internal stressors as well. Do you take in too much caffeine or alcohol? Do you abuse drugs? Do you overschedule your life so that you can't possibly do it all? The bad news is that chronic stress disrupts rejuvenating sleep, wreaks havoc on hormone levels, strains the cardiovascular system, impairs memory, causes emotional instability and conflict, saps the body of its normal healing abilities, and can even lead to premature aging. The good news is that stress can be managed, largely by adopting healthier lifestyle choices.

TYPES OF STRESS

The American Psychological Association (APA) acknowledges on its Web site that "stress management can be complicated and confusing because there are different types of stress—acute stress, episodic acute stress, and chronic stress—each with its own characteristics." There's also traumatic stress: what we feel after we've been through a natural disaster, had a serious accident, been a victim of violence, or suffered a sudden and extreme trauma. Posttraumatic stress is the delayed or chronic extension of that experience.

Acute Stress

According to the APA, the most common form of stress is acute stress. Stressors defined as acute are the things that ruin your plans or your day: a flat tire, a missed deadline, an unplanned meeting with your child's principal at school. The inevitable by-product of living, acute stress happens to everyone and tends to be manageable. These stressors don't do the damage of chronic stress, but they certainly affect your mind and body. This is the kind of stress that can easily be helped with the stress-management and relaxation techniques presented in this book.

Symptoms of Acute Stress
- *Emotional distress:* worry, anger, irritability, anxiety, depression, frustration, impatience
- *Physical problems:* fatigue; headache; back pain; jaw pain; trembling; cold hands and feet; and muscular stiffness that can lead to pulled muscles, tendons, and ligaments
- *Digestive problems:* heartburn, acid stomach, diarrhea, constipation, flatulence, irritable bowel syndrome
- *Vital-sign disturbances:* rise in blood pressure, rapid heartbeat, sweaty palms, heart palpitations, dizziness, cold extremities, shortness of breath, chest pain
- *Mental difficulties:* confusion, inability to concentrate, indecisiveness, mind racing, mindlessness, or blankness

Episodic Acute Stress

Everyone meets at least one stressor every day, but some people have a pattern of reacting as if everything is a big problem. These people experience acute stress more often. The classic type A personality is an example. According to Meter Friedman and Ray Rosenman, the cardiologists who coined the phrase, type A's have "an excessive competitive drive, aggressiveness, impatience, and a harrying sense of time urgency." They often have a "free-floating but well-rationalized form of hostility, and almost always a deep-seated insecurity." Acute stress seems to be a way of life for people like this.

12

"Worrywarts see disaster around every corner and pessimistically forecast catastrophe in every situation," say Lyle H. Miller, Ph.D., and Alma Dell Smith, Ph.D., authors of *The Stress Solution*. "The world is a dangerous, unrewarding, punitive place where something awful is always about to happen. These 'awfulizers' also tend to be overaroused and tense, but are more anxious and depressed than angry and hostile."

People who chronically worry and "catastrophize" have deep-seated patterns to address. "Often, lifestyle and personality issues are so ingrained and habitual with these individuals," say Miller and Smith, "that they see nothing wrong with the way they conduct their lives. They blame their woes on other people and external events. Frequently, they see their lifestyle, their patterns of interacting with others, and their ways of perceiving the world as part and parcel of who and what they are."

When the pain and discomfort of episodic acute stress get in the way of life as usual, that's the time to seek out stress management, often in the form of professional intervention.

Symptoms of Episodic Acute Stress

In addition to symptoms of acute stress:

- Persistent tension and migraine headaches
- Hypertension
- Asthma
- Chest pain
- Heart disease

Chronic Stress

Miller and Smith define chronic stress as "the grinding stress that wears people away day after day, year after year. Chronic stress destroys bodies, minds, and lives. It wreaks havoc through long-term attrition. It's the stress of poverty, of dysfunctional families, of being trapped in an unhappy marriage, or in a despised job or career. It's the stress that the never-ending 'troubles' have brought to the people of Northern Ireland, the tensions of the Middle East have brought to the Arabs and Jews, and the endless ethnic rivalries have brought to the people of Eastern Europe and the former Soviet Union." Chronic stress also affects people living in neighborhoods taken over by drug dealers and gang members. It often results in hopelessness and an inability to see a way out of "unrelenting demands and pressures for seemingly interminable periods of time," according to the APA.

Psychologists say chronic stress can result from childhood traumas that become internalized and affect a person's belief system and personality. Trying to mend the damage from this kind

13

Symptoms of Chronic Stress
- Loss of appetite, or overeating
- Diminished coping ability
- Feelings of insecurity and inadequacy
- Depression
- Weakened immune system
- Hypertension (if predisposed)
- Chronic fatigue
- Heart disease
- Migraine headaches
- Chronic pain in joints, back, jaw, or shoulders
- Persistent anxiety
- Pessimism
- Reclusiveness
- Resentment
- Constant irritability
- Extreme or chronic anger
- Cynicism
- Inability to concentrate
- Low performance levels
- Peptic ulcers
- Digestive disorders

14

of experience requires professional help and a commitment to deep self-examination.

"The worst aspect of chronic stress," say Miller and Smith, "is that people get used to it. They forget it's there. People are immediately aware of acute stress because it is new; they ignore chronic stress because it is old, familiar, and sometimes, almost comfortable. . . .

"Chronic stress kills through suicide, violence, heart attack, stroke, and, perhaps, even cancer. . . . People wear down to a final, fatal breakdown. Because physical and mental resources are depleted through long-term attrition, the symptoms of chronic stress are difficult to treat and may require extended medical as well as behavioral treatment and stress management."

Traumatic Stress and Posttraumatic Stress

Even when people have not sustained physical injury with traumatic stress, it often results in extreme emotional responses. Immediately after such an occurrence, there is often shock and denial. The shock can make you dazed and the denial is a coping mechanism—you can't believe what happened and you are putting off feeling its intensity. Traumatic and posttraumatic stress can have powerful, long-term effects that eat away at people's ability to recover from daily stressors. They may not even be aware that they are carrying this burden until they "snap" or become ill.

Posttraumatic stress can also be carried for years as baggage left over from childhood. This chronic stress can lay dormant for years and then lead to what seem like arbitrary overreactions to later problems. It can also undermine your health and peace of mind without your being aware of it. Professional help is indicated, but you can help yourself overcome posttraumatic stress with journaling, group rap sessions, relaxation practices, and other forms of self-exploration.

15

Professional help comes in many forms and you must choose the one that's right for you.

- Behavior therapy (to modify and control unwanted behaviors)
- Cognitive therapy (to change your unproductive thought patterns and reactions)
- Relaxation techniques (to quell anxiety and resolve stressors)
- Medication

Whether or not you need professional help after extreme trauma, it is important to acknowledge the experience and allow yourself time to heal. Give yourself permission to accept that you've been through something difficult. Be patient with yourself while you grieve. Realize you will experience emotional ups and downs. If you can, avoid making any major changes in your life for a while, particularly those concerning career or relationships.

Communication is extremely important when dealing with traumatic stress. Ask for support from family and friends, and be compassionate and patient when dealing with others who have gone through the same trauma with you. Support groups are excellent outlets; it's best to find those led by trained, experienced professionals, although nonprofessional Twelve Step groups like Alcoholics Anonymous are successful and reputable. Keeping a journal or diary is also a productive way to express your thoughts and emotions.

After a traumatic experience, it's even more crucial to pursue healthy lifestyle habits that counter everyday stressors. Eat nutritious, well-balanced meals; avoid stimulants and depressants such as alcohol and tobacco; exercise regularly; allow yourself plenty of rest and try to maintain a regular sleeping routine; pursue your hobbies and deliberately create playtimes; and practice relaxation techniques.

Normal Responses to Traumatic Stress
- *Feelings:* unpredictable, intense mood swings; anxiety; nervousness; depression
- *Thoughts:* flashbacks; vivid memory of the event; inability to concentrate
- *Physical reactions:* rapid heartbeat; sweating; headache, nausea, chest pain, general pain, and digestive problems
- *Relationship problems:* strained, frequent arguments with family members and/or coworkers; withdrawal and isolation from group activity

EFFECTS OF STRESS

Living with continued stress without using relaxation and stress management to regain a balance will surely cause the body to rebel. Numerous medical studies show a connection between stress and heart disease, ulcers, and skin conditions. The following are but some of the physical problems brought on by stress.

Immunity

At Ohio State University (OSU), Professors Janice K. Kiecolt-Glaser, Ph.D., and Ronald Glaser, Ph.D., have done ground-breaking research on the effects of stress on the immune system. They have demonstrated that stress plays a role in lessening the effectiveness of vaccines, lowering immune systems in cancer patients, slowing dental wound healing, and much more. Philip Marucha, associate professor of periodontology at OSU, did a study with Kiecolt-Glaser, published in *Psychosomatic Medicine,* which concluded that stress can lengthen the time wounds take to heal by as much as 40 percent. He said the study was important because "wound healing plays a vital role in how the body responds to every infection we get, regardless of its location."

Studies with mice showed that social stress could cause a dormant herpes virus to resurface. And a 1991 study by Sheldon Cohen, Ph.D., of Carnegie Mellon University, injected hundreds of healthy people with a cold virus and found that those who reported more stress in their lives were more likely to get sick.

"Recent research shows that persons who are under both short-term and long-term life stress have negative changes in immune system function, including delayed healing of wounds to the skin," says William R. Novallo, associate director of the MacArthur Foundation Research Network on Mind–Body Interactions and professor of psychiatry and behavioral sciences at the University of Oklahoma. Novallo's foundation is supporting a Network on Socioeconomic Status and Health that is looking into influences on health, stress included.

Insomnia and Pain

Millions of Americans suffer from insomnia and chronic pain, two widespread conditions that often result from or are exacerbated by stress. Individuals and their families suffer the consequences from the resulting disabilities and lost productivity.

Insomnia can be the cause of stress or the result of it. It has been reported that at least one-third and perhaps as much as half of the U.S. population suffers from some form of insomnia. If you are anxious, nervous, depressed, bored, or lonely, or are suffering from disease or injury, you may have problems getting enough sleep. Excess intake of caffeine, drugs, or alcohol can cause insomnia. But studies have documented improvements in insomniacs who embrace relaxation techniques such as massage, deep breathing, yoga, meditation, light therapy, aromatherapy, visualization, self-hypnosis, and herbology.

Pain is a physiological reaction: If you cut yourself or break a bone, nerve cells send chemical signals to your brain. But this involuntary reaction can be "magnified or diminished by emotion," says Peter S. Staats, M.D., on discoveryhealth.com. "A patient might come in with tremendous pain, thinking she has cancer," he writes. "Once she discovers the pain is only due to a pulled muscle, the pain decreases almost immediately." Even for people who do have cancer, at least one study found that mood is related to life expectancy.

In 1995, the NIH National Center for Complementary and Alternative Medicine and the NIH Office of Medical Applications and Research sponsored a conference called "Integration of Behavioral and Relaxation Approaches into the

19

Treatment of Chronic Pain and Insomnia." The panel found strong evidence that relaxation techniques are effective in treating many chronic pain conditions, such as low back pain and arthritis. Conventional medicine (drugs and surgery) has had limited success with such chronic conditions; the panel encouraged wider acceptance of alternative approaches as treatments. Practices such as the relaxation response, hypnosis, biofeedback, and cognitive behavioral techniques were cited as helpful for the treatment of chronic pain associated with some cancers, irritable bowel syndrome, mouth inflammation, temporomandibular joint disorders, insomnia, and tension headaches.

20

Premature Aging

When one's whole being is compromised by unmanaged stress, it can lead to exhaustion, depression, and signs of premature aging. One of the reasons that the holistic approach to wellness of mind, body, and spirit is taking off is the baby boomers' refusal to accept stereotypical notions of "old age." Nutrition, exercise, stress management, and spirituality all contribute greatly to one's biological age irrespective of actual chronological age. Research continues unabated into how this occurs. For example, a 1999 article in the journal *Neurology* reported that French researchers kept tabs on the blood pressure and mental status of 1,172 people ages fifty-nine to seventy-one. They found that those who had uncontrolled high blood pressure showed significant decline in mental function. And a 1998 Swedish study found that men with untreated high blood pressure had more cases of dementia.

As director of OSU's Clinical Research Center, William B. Malarkey, M.D., has been involved with the stress and immunity studies of Kiecolt-Glaser and Glaser for many years. He has also worked as a practicing physician for more than thirty years. Malarkey says that negative stressors affect every facet of our physical and psychological health, including how well we age and how long we live. In his book *Take Control of Your Aging,* he describes what he calls the PIERS (Physical, Intellectual, Emotional, Relational, Spiritual) program, which he feels will allow people to live longer and better. Because he knows negative stress affects the immune system so greatly, Malarkey practices what he preaches. He exercises every day, and enjoys tandem biking and kayaking with his wife. He opts for good nutrition, and practices breathing techniques when stuck in traffic. "I've studied the effects of stress on the immune system, so I have learned to monitor myself to include self-corrections when I'm in the midst of stress," he says.

One of the most important considerations for Malarkey is the spiritual component. "I spend some time every day doing something for spiritual inoculation," he says. "We need to remember that we are human beings, not human doings," he's fond of saying. "I don't believe there is such a thing as an inconsequential thought." Every minute you ruminate on unresolved bad events of the past can hurt you. "If you spend some time in solitude, and reflecting and meditating on your positive spiritual side, that can contribute to a longer and better life." He also believes having many friends and doing things for others contribute positively.

21

Changing the way we react to stress is vital. "We are all like the insect I see on my window, repeatedly traversing the glass seeking a way out but unaware of the possibilities of freedom, even after I have opened the latch," Malarkey says. "Finally a breeze convinces him of new opportunities, and he stretches his wings and flies away. Many of us are trapped in myths and behaviors that are influencing the quality of our lives and are placing us on a rapid slope of decline. We would like the freedom of escaping from certain behaviors but have been unwilling to take the risk of spreading our wings and taking flight."

AIDS

"Faster progression to AIDS was associated with more cumulative stressful life events, more cumulative depressive symptoms, and less cumulative social support," according to a study published in *Psychosomatic Medicine*, the journal of the American Psychosomatic Society. Jane Leserman, Ph.D., led a team of researchers who examined the effects of stress and social support on the progression of HIV infection. The researchers studied eighty-two HIV-infected gay men who had no symptoms of AIDS at baseline, for up to five and a half years. After adjusting for age, education, race, CD4+ count, tobacco use, and medications, the study concluded that the disease was accelerated in the men who felt more stressed and had fewer sources of moral support.

At the University of Miami, Michael Antoni, Ph.D., associate professor of psychology and psychiatry, found that asymptomatic HIV-infected men who underwent stress-management training showed a slower rate of decline in the immunological cells that attack the AIDS virus than did men who received no such training.

At the University of Miami, Gail Ironson, M.D., Ph.D., studied the effects of massage on men with HIV-weakened immune systems. After receiving massages five days a week for a month, the men's immune functions demonstrably improved.

Infertility

The effects of stress management on infertility have been investigated by Alice D. Domar, Ph.D., director of the Mind/Body Center for Women's Health at the Mind/Body Medical Institute, assistant professor of medicine at Harvard Medical School, and author of *Self-Nurture: Learning to Care for Yourself as Effectively as You Care for Everyone Else.* Domar studied women who were unable to conceive and had tried every possible solution. Her clinical workshop was meant to help the women come to terms with the fact they couldn't get pregnant, but the stress-management techniques she taught them led to some surprising results. After six months, 44 percent of the 174 women she tracked had achieved conception, and 60 percent of the women who had been identified as severely depressed had conceived.

Women's Health

As a spokesperson for the American Heart Association's "Take Wellness to Heart" campaign, noted author and poet Maya Angelou says, "We have to look after our own health—those of us who have so long looked after the health of others."

The Society for Women's Health Research is concerned with "gender-based biology, the field of scientific inquiry committed to identifying the biological and physiological differences between men and women." Depression is two to three times more common in women than in men, in part because women's brains make less of the calming hormone serotonin. Practicing relaxation techniques can increase serotonin levels.

In August 1998, *Stroke*, one of five journals published by the American Heart Association, reported that women who exhibit large increases in blood pressure and heart rate during mental stress may develop accelerated atherosclerosis, the disease that obstructs blood vessels and can trigger heart attack or stroke. The lead author of the study, Karen Matthews, Ph.D., of the University of Pittsburgh, says, "If women have a large pulse pressure response to stress, then they should consider stress management."

Eating Disorders

Although there is a small percentage of men who have eating disorders, more women suffer from such conditions. It appears that anorexia, bulimia, and compulsive overeating could be positively affected by relaxation techniques that encourage the release of serotonin, according to a study by Philip Cowen, M.D., F.R.C.Psych., of Oxford University, and Walter Kaye, M.D., University of Pittsburgh. "Serotonin pathways are involved in the regulation of eating and mood," Cowen says in the February 1999 *Archives of General Psychiatry*. "In certain vulnerable people, a lowering of serotonin can result in depression and appetite deregulation."

People with eating disorders should seek professional help. This may include nutritional and psychological counseling. Patients will find that stress-management practices like those in this book will be advised for regular practice. According to the National Association of Anorexia Nervosa and Associated Disorders, "General relaxation exercises, guided imagery, self-hypnosis, meditation, or any relaxation technique may help to reduce or relieve anxieties. Regular practice of these techniques at times of stress may have some effect on reducing the impact of stressful incidents."

Heart Health

Coronary heart disease is the number one killer of men and women in the United States. Experts say that of the estimated half-million deaths each year, a great number could be avoided with lifestyle changes. Although heredity plays a role, there are controllable factors such as blood pressure, weight, substance abuse and smoking, physical inactivity, and stress management.

Current research about the prevention of heart disease focuses not only on cholesterol, nutrition, blood pressure, and exercise but also on the mind, body, and spirit as well. As research has shown the negative physical effects of mental stress, setting aside time for relaxation has been shown to promote a healthy heart.

Research on mental stress and myocardial ischemia shows that mental stress can cause ischemic (lack of blood flow due to arterial obstruction) episodes in the same way as physical overexertion. Studies showed that people with coronary artery disease who received stress-management training were at considerably reduced risk of ischemic attack than those who were treated with standard care or also with exercise programs. And a study at the University of Pittsburgh showed a relationship between extreme reactions to mental stress and high blood pressure, which is a risk factor for atherosclerosis (buildup and hardening of fatty deposits on the inside of blood vessels, which can result in heart attack and stroke).

Dean Ornish, M.D., has done some pioneering work in demonstrating that heart disease can not only be stopped but also be reversed with a holistic program that includes stress reducers such as yoga and meditation, along with cardiovascular exercise and a specific nutrition program. He has incorporated this knowledge into many books and tapes, including *Dr. Dean Ornish's Program for Reversing Heart Disease* and *The Healing Power of Intimacy*.

Ornish says that medical science has given credence to the value of a holistic approach to healing and that better health is available to almost anyone who is open to a new direction. In an address to the International Spa Association in 1994, he cited a cartoon in which several dinosaurs were looking up at the sky as snow began to fall. "If we [who practice traditional medicine] don't recognize a changing atmosphere and do something about it," Ornish said, "we'll end up just like the dinosaurs."

26

Memory

"If it's been a really, really tough week at work and you can't remember where you put your car keys, it may be that high levels of the stress hormone cortisol are interfering with your memory," say representatives of the Washington University School of Medicine on its Web site, "Science Daily." The good news is that research by John W. Newcomer, M.D., associate professor of psychiatry and psychology, indicates that it would take several days of such stresses as major surgery or severe psychological trauma to produce memory impairment. With respite, your cortisol levels can return to normal.

Produced by the body when stressed, cortisol is one of the family of stress hormones called glucocorticoids. In his research, Newcomer compared the memory and cognitive functions of people who were given a high dose, a low dose, or a placebo. Memory impairment was observed only in the high-dose group, and that improved after some time off the cortisol.

27

MINDFULNESS

Perhaps as a reaction to "techno-overload," society is beginning to look at time-outs and changing perspective as ways of coping. Zen is a very old concept of Mahayana Buddhism that aims at enlightenment by direct intuition through meditation. To simplify, Zen masters strive through meditation to be in the moment, clear the mind of conscious thought, and breathe deeply and rhythmically.

The Zen concept of this time-out, seated meditation called *zazen* includes an attempt not to think with the mind but to exist in the body. In spas and seminars, the Zen concept of mindfulness has been adapted to mean being completely tuned in to the activity of the moment. If you are working, give yourself up to it. If you are holding your loved ones, don't think about work.

Mindfulness Meditation

Studies have shown that mindfulness meditation or "insight meditation," based on Buddhist tradition, decreases anxiety and
increases the pain threshold. Research by Jon Kabat-Zinn, Ph.D.,
in mind–body medicine also investigated the effects of mindfulness meditation on chronic pain, stress-related disorders, chronic
diseases such as cancer, psychosocial stress related to poverty and
associated social conditions, inmates and correctional institutions,
work-related stress, and athletic performance enhancement.
Kabat-Zinn developed a system called "Mindfulness-Based Stress
Reduction" that is taught at centers throughout the country.

28

Contemporary psychological approaches often integrate
principles of this Zen philosophy. Gestaltist Fritz Perls defines
anxiety as "any time you leave the present." Except for cases of
unusual trauma, on most of the occasions in which you get
upset, you are in fact reacting to your history of such situations
or projecting into the future, rather than experiencing what is
happening in the moment.

When you stay in the moment, you can moderate inappropriate stress reactions as they are happening. If you concentrate on "being there" while meditating or doing breathing
exercises, you are able to deflect unnecessary thoughts to clear
the "brain noise" and allow your body to benefit from the calming and healing effects of relaxation. You can learn to observe
your unconscious reactions, which can shed light on why you
react as you do, and this can lead to the awareness that you can
have a choice as to how you react to stressors.

Spas, New Age retreats, and yoga centers have been teaching different forms of meditation for decades. More and more

wellness clinics, hospitals, and university medical centers are making such classes and seminars available. In fact, the department of psychiatry at Columbia-Presbyterian Medical Center in New York City opened the Center for Meditation and Healing in 1998. "What we do here in complementary psychiatry combines the best of modern psychiatry with time-tested meditative traditions," says Joseph Loizzo, M.D., the center's director. "Our aim is to foster self-care by offering health education that allows participants to learn, grow, and change. The ultimate goal is to support and teach people so they become more independent and develop self-healing attitudes, habits, and skills."

STRESS-RESISTANT PERSONALITIES

In a Harvard Medical School study, Raymond Flannery Jr., Ph.D., found that people who handle stress well have important coping skills in common:

- They take personal control.
- They are involved in something meaningful to them.
- They are committed to a goal.
- They make wise lifestyle choices: get regular exercise, relax for at least fifteen minutes each day, avoid artificial stimulants, and eat nutritiously.
- They actively seek the company of others.
- They have a sense of humor.
- They espouse spiritual values.

Project SMART (Stress Management and Relaxation Training), an outgrowth of Flannery's studies, teaches coping skills to bolster stress resistance. Flannery says, "By following a modified diet, doing aerobic exercise three times a week for twenty minutes, reaching out to people, taking personal responsibility for our decisions, showing concern for others, and keeping a sense of humor, you can utilize the skills of people who seem to naturally be more able to withstand the stresses of life."

AGE-OLD TRADITIONS

Alternative medicine and relaxation therapies are practices that have been used for centuries by other cultures all over the world. In Native American, Asian, and Indian traditions, for example, the holistic approach is nothing new. The theory is based on the assumption that a human is affected by factors that impede the natural flow of energy—called *qi* or *chi* in the Orient—through the body. Negative stressors on body, mind, and spirit can arise from any number of conditions. When energy flow is blocked, the body's balance is disturbed and can result in ill health, low spirits, stress, and anxiety. Freeing the energy flow restores harmony as well as the body's ability to maintain its immune system and emotional balance.

Oriental Medicine

Eastern medical practitioners say all disease reflects a disharmony of the body's yin and yang. Although you often hear yin–yang being described as female–male representations, the original meanings were bright side–dark side, according to Richard A.

30

Feely, D.O. "Everything in the world can be described, explained, and further divided into the yin–yang phenomena," he says. A college professor, physician, and senior clinician at American Whole Health in Chicago, Feely's Oriental medicine Web site discusses the philosophy and diagnostic tools of this tradition. Oriental medicine, says Feely, is a complex holistic system that recognizes the significance of The Five Elements, which have yin and yang characteristics that interact within all of nature. These elements are fire, earth, metal, water, and wood. Taoist student and Chi Nei Tsang therapist Dennis Lewis says these five elements "symbolically express the five phases or movements of energy." When one element overcontrols another, it must be counteracted with an intervention.

In the Taoist philosophy, life depends on the harmony of yin and yang and the five elements. In humans they manifest as three energies or Three Treasures (*jing,* sexual energy; *chi,* vitality; and *shen,* spirit), says Lewis. "Through the work of self-awareness and inner alchemy, it is possible to increase the natural transformation of jing into chi, and chi into shen, for spiritual growth as well as good health."

Imbalances are diagnosed according to colors, emotions, flavors, senses, climates, body parts, and organs, which are all related to the five elements. These can be observed by skin or tongue color, pulse, body palpitation, listening, smelling, and questioning by practitioners of Chinese medicine, who may recommend a traditional cure such as acupuncture, herbs, heat, acupressure, qigong, massage, or other therapies.

For example, "Anxiety is an emotion that Oriental medicine generally associates with the organ system of the heart and

31

liver," say Boaz Brizman, D.Ac., and Matia Brizman, D.Ac. By treating these organ systems with acupuncture, anxiety may be lessened or eradicated.

Acupuncture

Acupuncture is the use of small needles inserted just under the skin into energy points called "meridians." It has been a component of traditional Chinese medicine for thousands of years. It is said to free internal energy flow (chi), which relieves pain and allows the body to heal itself.

Acupuncture has been practiced since at least 500 B.C. in China; some historians say the technique was used as far back as 2500 B.C. According to Feely, the Dutch East Indian Trading Company introduced Chinese acupuncture to Europe. Egypt, Greece, and Rome "recorded clinical uses of earrings and other forms of ear stimulation for various problems, particularly in the treatment of sexual and menstrual disorders."

The theory is that the needles correct blockages or imbalances of the body's energy flow that, if uncorrected, can lead to disease. Much of the research has centered around chronic or postoperative pain management, but acupuncture is being studied as a primary or alternative therapy for a wide variety of conditions including substance addiction, stroke rehabilitation, headache, menstrual cramps, tennis elbow, fibromyalgia, muscle pain, arthritis, back pain, carpal tunnel syndrome, asthma, and depression.

"Acupuncture is used to harmonize the body's physiological responses to stressors in one's life," says Feely. "Since it is known to activate the production of neuroproteins in the brain—endorphins, enkephalins, dymorphine, and others—balance and peace can be physiologically restored to the nervous system and the spirit."

Ayurveda

Ayurveda (from the Sanskrit *ayu* [life] and *veda* [knowledge]) is a way of life used to promote well-being through maintaining balance. A holistic Indian tradition that has been practiced for more than five thousand years, in Ayurveda, philosophy and medicine are not separate entities, and attention to mind, body, and spirit includes yoga, meditation, massage, and diet. A purification ritual called panchakarma is recommended several times a year. In Ayurveda all matter is considered to be made up of The Five Elements. They do not exist as isolated forms but as combinations in which one or more elements are dominant.

Ayurveda sees three body types, or energies, in the human body. These are called doshas. Each dosha is comprised of three main combinations of the five elements. The three doshas are kapha, pitta, and vata. When you are out of balance, disharmony produces stress and illness.

"According to Ayurveda," says Melanie Sachs, certified Ayurvedic lifestyle counselor, teacher, and therapist, "stress is the root cause of all health problems. Stress causes indigestion, which in turn causes all manner of energetic imbalances.

"With stress due to poor digestion, environmental pollution, physical or mental trauma, time pressures, and other factors, the vital energy system, or marma, of the body begins to

33

The Three Ayurvedic Doshas

- Kapha-dominant individuals are most often healthy, content, calm, and soft-spoken; tend to have a large frame and well-developed body; are slow, graceful, quiet; have trouble maintaining desirable weight; often become possessive, greedy, and envious when under stress; and are prone to colds, flu, and seasonal allergies.
- Pitta-dominant individuals typically have moderate body size and activity level; are measured, purposeful, and direct; are strong willed and ambitious; tend to exhibit short temper, irritability, and aggression under stress; and are more prone to skin problems and intolerance to sun and heat.
- Vata-dominant individuals are usually physically active; tend to be thin; are quick and light on their feet; may become indecisive, insecure, fearful, and anxious when under stress; and are more prone to digestive and colon problems.

malfunction," Sachs says. "On a physical level, this leads to tissues being poorly nourished. . . . On a mental level, it leads to us making less health-supportive choices, i.e., grabbing a cup of coffee instead of relaxing or taking a nap. On a spiritual level, we become disconnected from our sense of greater purpose or higher good, and we lose inspiration."

Ayurveda uses massage as an important part of reawakening the marma system. Everyone must be treated with regard to their own doshas and environmental considerations: "One man's meat may well be another's poison," says Sachs. "For example, gentle exercise is very beneficial for kapha-dominant individuals, while rest and relaxation is more nourishing to those more vata dominant."

The National Institute of Ayurvedic Medicine is working with medical institutions to substantiate the benefits of the Ayurvedic approach. Researchers at the Richard and Hinda Rosenthal Center for Alternative and Complementary Medicine in New York are studying Ayurvedic herbal medicines for women's conditions such as perimenopause, premenstrual syndrome, and painful menstruation. At the National Cancer Institute in Bethesda, Maryland, they are studying antitumor effects. In New Delhi, India, the Central Council for Research in Ayurveda and Siddha Medicine is assessing the use of Ayurvedic herbs, yoga, and meditation for asthma. Other studies are being done with Ayurveda on the immune system, serum cholesterol levels, depression, chronic fatigue syndrome, hypertension, diabetes, and herpes. Using multiple modalities, research is being done on obesity, uterine fibroids, acne, irritable bowel syndrome, chronic constipation, and other diseases.

Some wellness clinics specialize in the Ayurvedic approach. The Chopra Center for Well Being in La Jolla, California, offers Ayurvedic body therapies on its menus, as do many day and destination spas.

35

Do-It-Yourself Ayurvedic Head Massage: Shirobhyanga

AIM: To refresh the mind and body, relieve tension and fatigue, and improve complexion. (This massage can be done with oil as an Ayurvedic beauty treatment.) "Massaging the head will increase fresh oxygen and glucose supply to the brain, and improve circulation of the spinal fluid around the brain and spinal cord," says certified Ayurvedic lifestyle counselor Melanie Sachs. "It also increases the release of hormones and enzymes necessary for the growth of the brain and relaxation of the body. Head massage is particularly beneficial before bathing in the morning to gently awaken the nerves. In the evening it helps remove the stresses of the day and promotes peaceful sleep." It will relieve muscle tension, too.

Step One
Point 1 is at the crown of the head on the midline. To find it easily and accurately, put your right hand over your forehead, with the heel of the hand at the top of your nose, three fingers pointing up over your head. With your left hand, measure three fingers' width back from the tip of the middle finger of your right hand. This is the crown point, or "Mardhi" marma in Ayurveda, the most therapeutic point on the head where blood vessels, nerves, and lymphatics meet. Kapha, pitta, and vata doshas meet here as well.

All marma points should be touched with great care, rubbing in gentle, small, clockwise circles, gradually increasing, then gradually releasing pressure, spiraling in and spiraling out. (If you are applying warm oil, massage this marma point for thirty to sixty seconds, or for thirty-five clockwise circles.)

Step Two
Point 2 is three fingers' width in front of the crown point, still on the midline. This marma is called the "Brahma Randra." Massage, with or without oil, as in Step One.

Step Three
Point 3 is four fingers' width behind the crown point. It is called the "Shiva Randra" marma. Massage again as in Step One.

Step Four
With the index and middle fingers of your right hand, find the bony bump behind your right earlobe, the "Karna" marma. Using those fingers make small circles, progressing along the ridge of the skull toward the base of your neck, where your large neck muscles meet your skull. Switch to your left hand, and proceed up to the same bony point behind your left ear. Work back down the center of your neck again, and switch hands back up to your right ear. Repeat this back-and-forth massage path two more times. You will also be touching the "Manya" marmas in the process.

37

Marmaveda

Another form of Ayurvedic tradition is Marmaveda, the science of universal electromagnetic energy. "In the Indian tradition, the generator of the life energy, or 'shakti,' is known as the 'kundalini,'" says Joseph Kurian, master of Marma science, author of *Living in Beauty*, and formulator of a line of Marmavedic beauty products. "The West is more familiar with the idea that everyone has an inner light. It is the same idea. This inner light is carried through the marma channels, which regulate the energy flow to all areas of the body."

A Marmaveda Breathing Technique

Preparation: Choose a comfortable sitting position and keep your spine straight; cross-legged or on your knees and calves are good. Determine which nostril is open or closed by putting a finger on a nostril. If one is closed, or only partially open, this indicates the hemisphere of the brain opposite to that nostril is not functioning optimally, and the electromagnetic current is not being efficiently produced by the body's generator, bringing fatigue. To open the nostril and increase the flow of air, take a deep breath, then breath out alternately through each nostril. Repeat three times; that should open the nose.

The exercise: With your spine straight, gently press the right side of the nose with the thumb of the right hand, and close the right nostril. Slowly inhale through the left nostril, until the lungs are full. This practice should be extremely slow and gentle. After inhaling, retain the air in the lungs. Then close the left nostril with both the third and fourth fingers of your right hand, and breathe out slowly and completely through the right nostril. Breathe in through the right nostril, hold, close, and breathe out through the left nostril. Repeat this for twelve in-and-out breaths.

39

While doing this pranayama breathing technique, imagine the energy is going through the nostril to the hemisphere on the opposite side of the brain and up to the crown chakra at the top of your head. From there it descends to the kundalini, the center of your life energy, at the base of your spine. As you hold your breath, have in your awareness that the energy is moving up and down your body and stopping briefly at each chakra [see page 108]. As the breath goes out, follow its energy with your mind until the impurities are released from the body. Repeat this mental pattern as you breathe in through the opposite nostril. Each time you inhale, your breath is waking up the eight marmas connected to the chakras.

From *Living in Beauty* by Joseph Kurian (EMC Publishing, 2000). Used with permission.

Kurian says this energy exists everywhere, in all life-forms, and they interact in a powerful way. "If there is blockage in the marmas, imbalance occurs. By removing blockages in the marmas, we have the potential to maintain our body, mind, and spirit exactly as nature intended."

Blockages occur over time from accidents and stress. The marmas are also susceptible to environmental influences such as air, food, seasonal change, and even electromagnetic vibrations, according to Kurian. "The constitution of the body can change when the marmas are imbalanced. When they are corrected, the constitution balances. . . . The key to physical and mental well-being is keeping all energy channels open for the marmas to conduct the transmission of vital life force."

Kurian says using Marmavedic mudras—or postures that connect energy points to complete a circuit—can facilitate "the flow of life force." When you touch your thumb with any finger, it corresponds to each of the five major organs: You are harmonizing the balance of the brain and that organ, creating a path between them. When you touch your thumb to the forefinger, it represents the lungs; the middle finger represents the intestines; the ring finger, the kidneys; the pinky finger, the heart. That's why meditators often touch the thumb and a finger together while sitting in the lotus position.

Marmaveda uses herbology in teas and topical preparations, along with diet, massage, exercise, breathing, meditation, and other Ayurvedic techniques, to promote healing and optimize well-being.

40

FINDING A RELAXATION THERAPY

As Dr. Benson says, all practices that are mindfully meant to relax you will provide stress relief. Try a few on for size, and see which is most comfortable for you. Although certain practices may be emotionally or spiritually uncomfortable for some, everyone can find something effective and suitable. Remember, the goal of the precious time you make for yourself in a busy day is to make you feel better. If, after experimenting with a technique, it doesn't seem to fit, try another, and another. You may settle on just one, or rotate practices depending on your mind/body/spirit state.

Finding a Stress-Management Therapist

If you want to try some of the relaxation and stress-management practices that require a professional therapist, there are some things to consider.

As any contemporary consumer knows, you should do your homework. Get some recommendations from your doctor or close friends, if possible.

Alternative therapies can counter disease, demonstrating relief from everything from arthritis to ulcers. However, if you have a disease or any medical conditions for which you are being treated and/or taking medication, you must inform your stress-management therapist. A good therapist will always start with questions about your health, concerns, and goals. If those questions are not forthcoming, don't sit quietly. Be sure to bring up the subjects yourself if you have an otherwise good impression of the therapist. If you don't get a good impression, try another therapist.

Most relaxation therapies will not harm you, but those administered by trained professionals will be more effective and provide longer-lasting effects. Those who suffer from heart disease, diabetes, circulatory problems, or high blood pressure, and women who are pregnant, can all benefit greatly by practicing relaxation techniques, but there are some things they should be aware of and should discuss with their doctors before starting a new practice. Heat treatments such as hydrotherapy, steam rooms, and saunas should be avoided by people with these conditions. Certain types of massage, such as aromatherapy, involve potent herbs and oils that can interfere with a medication's effects, or may be irritating to people with allergies or sensitive skin. Swollen or injured areas should be touched only by massage therapists who specialize in injuries (and probably should be avoided during the session). Before taking herbal and nutritional supplements, they should be carefully investigated in regard to your specific condition, and for any adverse drug interactions.

No relaxation therapy should be used as a primary treatment for disease or as an alternative to surgery. Your doctors should know about your stress therapies, and your relaxation counselors should know about your doctors' treatments.

Feel free to ask questions about the therapy: what you'll expect to happen during the session, how long it will take to feel the benefits, what the alternatives are. Could a therapy have any negative effects on your condition? Find out if your insurance covers alternative therapies. Don't be embarrassed to ask about the costs of treatment sessions; sometimes there is a discount for a series of treatments.

Ask a potential therapist about his or her training, certification, and professional affiliations. You can check with your state's licensing boards and consumer affairs departments about whether practitioners have had any complaints lodged against them.

An important consideration is your comfort level. Follow your instincts. To maximize your time and money, your therapist should be someone with whom you feel safe and comfortable.

Except for people with deeply ingrained psychological problems requiring specialized, long-term treatment, therapeutic techniques should be adaptable for home practice. Discuss with your potential therapist how that can be accomplished.

The NIH National Center for Complementary and Alternative Medicine (NCCAM) conducts and supports basic and applied research and training, and disseminates information on complementary and alternative medicine to practitioners and the public.

NCCAM does not serve as a referral agency for various alternative medical treatments or individual practitioners. NCCAM facilitates and conducts biomedical research.

The NIH cautions users not to seek the therapies described on its Web pages (see Resources, p. 210) without the consultation of a licensed health-care provider. Inclusion of a treatment or resource on the NCCAM Web site does not imply endorsement by the NCCAM, the NIH, or the Department of Health and Human Services.

43

CHILDREN AND STRESS

One of the miracles of childhood is that kids get upset easily but can just as easily return to a happy state. There are some acute episodic and chronic stresses in children, however, that serve as extra challenges for the whole family.

"School-related stress is the most prevalent, untreated cause of academic failure in our schools," says Ronald L. Rubenzer for the Educational Resources Information Center (ERIC) Clearinghouse on Handicapped and Gifted Children, in Reston, Virginia. "Achievement stress, the widespread 'invisible disability,' is rarely detected but generally gets worse as children progress through school. . . . Untreated achievement stress may result in academic failure, behavioral or emotional problems, drug abuse, health problems, and even suicide." He says learning-disabled children are at even greater risk because classmates can be insensitive, making these students less likely to participate fully in the educational and socializing experiences most children go through at school.

The government's ERIC Digest #452 suggests a "whole child" approach to help such children avoid becoming the type A's of tomorrow. Recommended techniques include many of the adult relaxation therapies included in this book: visualization, affirmation, positive thinking, time-out, relaxation exercises, and music and art therapy.

Alternative-style games and products for kids are hitting the market to help young people appreciate relaxation techniques. Of course, for children the products are presented as play. For example, Imaginazium has developed packages such as the

Yoga Kit for Kids with instruction guides, flash cards, and stickers, and an Empowerment Pack for Kids with game cards, a guided imagery tape, origami and activity guide, and stickers, based on color therapy.

Activities to inspire creativity and provide hobbies distinct from traditional pastimes like sports, dolls, and board games help broaden a child's mind, divert frustrating feelings, and allow quiet relaxation. For example, *Electric Bread: A Bread Machine Activity Book for Kids* combines art therapy and learning colors, shapes, and cooking for young minds and bodies.

There are bedtime relaxation tapes for tots, such as *The Floppy Sleep Game* and *The Sound of Dreams* from Dreamtime Productions. *Good Night* from Greathall Productions Inc. is an audiotape with vignettes that "bring feelings of safety and love" to bedtime with soothing music after each story. Stress-reducing music tapes aimed at young people are so popular now that they are frequently found at the checkout counters at children's stores and bookstores.

45

Teen Perspective

Adolescent girls and boys experience similar levels of stress, which tend to increase with age, but their distinctly different stress patterns may leave girls more vulnerable to depression. According to the August 1999 issue of *Child Development*, girls are more likely to be stressed over their relationships with parents, friends, and teachers; boys seem to stress over situations such as performance or trouble in school, moving to a new home, and other factors apart from relationships.

"Because adolescent girls may be more invested than boys in their relationships as a source of emotional support," says Karen D. Rudolph, M.D., of the University of Illinois, Champaign, "interpersonal stress may be more salient and may act as a stronger threat to their well-being."

When Bad Things Happen

When extreme trauma occurs, such as serious illness, family disruption, or natural disaster, the APA says there are steps parents and caregivers can take to alleviate the emotional consequences for children.

Give the children extra time and attention. Recognize that they may become more dependent than usual, and allow them to be. Hugging, kissing, and physical attention can be very comforting. Younger children often find it easier to work things out in play activities, such as role-playing with dolls or stuffed animals, or drawing pictures. Engage older children in heart-to-heart talks and make them feel safe when expressing their thoughts; encourage them to talk about their feelings. Invite their questions and try to answer with honesty, but recognize their age limitations and discuss things at an age-appropriate level, in terms they can understand. A counselor or religious advisor can be of help at this time.

Children of all ages may need a lot of extra reassurance and security. Keeping things as normal as possible, with the usual activities and schedule, is advisable. Let other caregivers such as teachers, baby-sitters, and sports coaches in on the situation.

As with adults under chronic stress, you'll know if it's time to seek out professional help. If children cannot return to normal in a reasonable amount of time; have continual emotional instability; become chronically aggressive, anxious, or angry; become withdrawn; or exhibit other extreme behaviors, that's the time to contact a mental-health professional.

2

The Mind/Body/Spirit Connection

Mind, body, and spirit are no longer looked upon as separate entities, and scores of clinical studies are demonstrating that all three must be nurtured to achieve and maintain good health. Experts agree that the basics of stress management are healthy nutrition, regular exercise, sufficient sleep, and mental relaxation.

If you want to alleviate the effects of stress, a good way to start is to commit yourself to some form of exercise. According to a recent study by the Surgeon General's office, "Physical activity has numerous physiologic effects. Most widely appreciated are its effects on the cardiovascular and musculoskeletal systems, but benefits on the functioning of metabolic, endocrine, and immune systems are also considerable."

When levels of good neurotransmitters such as serotonin are chronically depleted, depression can result. Some antidepressants, for example Prozac and Zoloft, are selective serotonin reuptake inhibitors. Relaxation techniques and regular exercise stimulate serotonin production and quell stress and anxiety in much the same way as these drugs.

Endorphins—the body's natural opiates—are part of a group of body-made chemicals that act on the central and peripheral nervous systems to suppress pain. Research shows that, in some people, endorphins may be involved in psychopathological behavior and that they seem to impact mood, immunity, addictiveness, and the general sense of well-being. Low endorphin levels can also contribute to premenstrual syndrome, which is why regular exercise, meditation, prayer, and relaxation training are prescribed for this condition.

50

EXERCISE

Exercise is vital to the health of our minds, bodies, and spirits. According to the aforementioned Surgeon General's report, "Physical activity appears to improve health-related quality of life by enhancing psychological well-being and by improving physical functioning in persons compromised by poor health."

You don't have to maintain an Olympic training schedule to reap the mental and physical benefits of exercise. It can take as little as thirty minutes of moderate daily activity. While golfing, walk the greens instead of taking the cart. Gardening is effective, if you're mowing and pruning actively. Dancing is a great, multidimensional therapy.

Swimming is a terrific overall exercise; it uses all your major muscle groups, and completing laps can be as aerobic as jogging. At the same time, it increases joint flexibility and is a good choice for people who want to avoid high-impact aerobics, which often do harm to the feet and knees. If you have been inactive or if you have a chronic condition such as cardiovascular disease or diabetes, see your physician before beginning any new exercise program. The Centers for Disease Control advises that you "start with moderate-intensity activity and gradually increase the duration and intensity until the goal (of thirty minutes of moderate activity almost daily) is reached." Be sure to include warm-up and cool-down periods before and after your workout.

A good physical fitness program will include aerobic exercise, strength training, and stretching. Join a gym, buy a workout video, plan lunchtime walks with a coworker, or set up evening activities with a loved one. There are jogging strollers for people with small children, chair exercise classes for people with disabilities, and dance and aerobics classes at community centers for people who hate jogging. There is no excuse for depriving yourself of the stress-countering benefits of exercise.

The Surgeon General's report cautions, "Many of the beneficial effects of exercise training—from both endurance and resistance activities—diminish within two weeks if physical activity is substantially reduced, and effects disappear within two to eight months if physical activity is not resumed." Of course, if you can stick with a new workout routine for a few weeks, you'll feel less stressed, and exercise will become second nature to you.

51

YOGA

Yoga (Sanskrit for *union*) is one of the best practices for the body and the mind. Studies have shown that yoga improves conditions as serious as arthritis, asthma, heart disease, and carpal tunnel syndrome. Yoga is noncompetitive and the increments of improvement are small but powerful.

Physically, the practice renews, invigorates, and heals the body. Muscles become toned and tightened, the internal organs and spine are guided into proper alignment for optimal function, and circulation is improved. Chronic muscle stress that results in back, neck, and shoulder pain is relieved. Flexibility, balance, and coordination also improve. Yoga is an ideal complement to all traditional forms of exercise. When performed properly, alignment and positions, called asanas, are much more important than how far you can bend or twist. The resulting deep relaxation and release of muscle tension is perfect as a stress-management technique.

Mentally, yoga increases body awareness and relieves chronic stress patterns. Because the practice of yoga helps you to center and sharpens your ability to concentrate, yoga will help you to counter stressful situations in everyday life as well. Committed yoga students also report heightened awareness, intuition, and creativity.

Despite pictures you may have seen of yoga practitioners who look like contortionists, Suza Francina, certified Iyengar instructor and author of *The New Yoga for People Over 50*, urges students to use common sense. "I especially want to caution readers not to strain their knees by attempting prematurely to sit in the Lotus posture or other bent-knee seated positions," she says. Iyengar uses props, wood blocks, and ropes to help the body max-

52

imize positions without strain. Francina claims yoga is the path to slowing the aging process, and has chapters in her book about menopause, osteoporosis, arthritis, joints, letting go of pain, and relaxation.

Types of Yoga

There are many styles of yoga, from gentle hatha yoga to the vigorous Astanga, a power yoga that will make you sweat. The styles are generally named after the leaders who developed them, but they all derive from Krishnamacharya, a legendary teacher at the Yoga Institute at the Mysore Palace in India.

Hatha yoga is a system practiced through the use of specific asanas.

Ananda yoga is a gentle style that prepares a student for meditation, directing the life force to organs and limbs.

Anusara yoga ("to step into the current of the Divine Will") is grounded in body alignment but is heart oriented and spiritual.

Astanga (or Ashtanga) is a system originated by K. Pattabhi Jois that uses six sequential, continuous-flow postures linked by dynamic breathing and motion.

In Bikram yoga, developed by Bikram Choudhury, twenty-six asanas are used to warm and stretch muscles, ligaments, and tendons in a particular order. Classes take place in a heated room.

Integral yoga, an integrated practice of postures, breathing, and meditation, was developed by Swami Satchidananda.

ISHTA is a vigorous and energizing yoga system combining meditation and breathing.

53

Iyengar, developed by B.K.S. Iyengar, emphasizes progressive alignment and precise action. It uses props such as blocks and belts to increase the body's range of motion and to train the mind to remain alert and focused.

Kali Ray (also called Tri Yoga) was developed by Kali Ray, and brings posture, breath, and focus together in flowing, sustained asanas that emphasize wavelike spinal motion. It can be gentle or challenging, according to ability.

Restorative yoga is a relaxing system that uses props such as bolsters, blankets, pillows, and blocks to support the body while stretching and breathing.

Sivananda, developed by Vishnu-devananda and named for his teacher, follows a set structure of breathing, classic postures, and meditation.

Viniyoga is a remedial, healing yoga based on the theory that body, emotion, attitude, diet, and behavior are connected to each other and to well-being.

Kripalu yoga is called the "yoga of consciousness" or "meditation in motion." Its gentle style can be adapted for students' different body types, ages, and physical needs. The emphasis is on correct breathing, body alignment, and coordinating breath and movement and "listening to your body." "It's a uniquely American form of hatha yoga that allows practitioners to experience deep relaxation, similar to what they would derive from sitting meditation, without having to sit," says Richard Faulds of The Kripalu Center for Yoga & Health in Lenox, Massachusetts. "Yoga works by breaking the cycle of stress and by balancing the sympathetic and parasympathetic nervous systems," he says. "If practiced daily, yoga helps practitioners avoid developing a pattern of chronic stress in the first place."

54

What to Look for in a Yoga Instructor
Tips from The Kripalu Center for Yoga
& Health

Look for
- teachers who have been trained and certified by a legitimate yoga training institute
- those who appear to understand anatomy
  and physiology
- those who have a gentle, attentive teaching style

Beware of
- teachers who have a cult following
- those who insist there is only one way
  to do a posture
- those who say "No pain, no gain"
- those who have a rude, abrupt, or harsh
  teaching style
- those who are stuck on the spiritual
  aspects to the exclusion of its physical
  value

55

Picking a yoga teacher is important. You should feel comfortable in the class, and reassured that you should be concentrating on your own progress and not comparing yourself to
classmates. People's body mechanics and natural ranges are different, so you may be improving yourself more than the person
on the next mat who appears to be more limber or have greater
range in a stretch. Good teachers will let you know that they are

observing you to make sure you interpret instructions correctly, and to monitor your breathing technique as carefully as your postures. The classroom should be clean, quiet, and dimly lit, to foster concentration and relaxation.

Yoga Tips from IDEA, The Health & Fitness Source

- Seek out a class appropriate to your fitness level and needs.
- Don't be afraid to ask your instructor to point out modifications to certain difficult poses, especially if you suffer from back or joint problems.
- In general, newcomers should avoid poses and moves that involve headstands, handstands, shoulder stands, the plough, and backward somersaults.
- If you suffer from glaucoma or high blood pressure, or are pregnant, discuss breathing techniques with your instructor to ensure these are not contraindicated.
- Start slowly with all new poses to avoid injury.

TAI CHI

Also known as tai chi chuan, this combination of yoga and meditation in motion has been practiced for hundreds of years, and groups practicing this resemble a human garden moving quietly, slowly, and deliberately in a kind of exercise ballet. Tai chi moves every part of the body, and is believed to be the way to long life and holistic health.

The Chinese characters for tai chi chuan can be translated as "supreme ultimate force." "Supreme ultimate" is associated with the philosophy of yin and yang, a dynamic duality in all things—dark–bright, male–female, active–passive. "Force" (literally "fist") is the way to achieve the supreme ultimate. Although the roots of tai chi are in martial arts, the choreographed forms or sets are practiced to stimulate the flow of chi in the body.

At the Johns Hopkins Medical Institutions in Baltimore, Maryland, a study suggests that tai chi can reduce blood pressure as much as regular aerobic exercise in older adults, without speeding up heart rate. Tai chi is also being studied by the NIH for its health benefits.

57

QIGONG

This Chinese practice is another slow-moving meditation to stimulate the body's energy. Also spelled "chi gong" and "chi kung," its name is derived from two Chinese words: *qui,* meaning "energy," and *gong,* meaning "skill" or "practice." Some say qigong is the oldest of Chinese arts, used as part of a religious system. This "skill of the energy/life force" has an internal component and external manifestation.

Here in the United States, qigong is used as a peaceful exercise and meditation technique. It can be spiritually uplifting and clarifying but is related to the personal belief system of the person performing it. Internally, qigong is similar to guided imagery (see chapter 3), with visualizations to move the energy inside the body. Externally, the practice includes movements with the meditation. Its physical benefits are those of other stress-management and relaxation therapies.

In China, research is being done about the effects of qigong on cancer treatment.

Yoga centers, spas, martial arts studios, acupuncture clinics, and community centers are places to seek out qigong classes.

SLEEP

You simply cannot function at your best if you are tired. Forty million Americans suffer from chronic sleep disorders and twenty to thirty million more have intermittent sleep-related problems, according to a 1998 report by the National Commission on Sleep Disorders Research.

Sleep disorders affect all age groups, and the consequences can be extreme. Falling asleep at the wheel and accidents in the workplace are among the worst-case scenarios.

Chronically stressed people usually suffer from fatigue. Most can function after the occasional sleepless night, but too many nights of tossing and turning lessen our ability to handle stressors.

No sleep, less resilience, more stress, less sleep—it's a vicious cycle. Each person's need for restful sleep can vary from five to ten hours a night; the average is seven to eight. If you get a good night's sleep, you'll wake refreshed, have adequate energy the next day, and wake naturally around the time an alarm clock would be set. Based on that criteria, do you think you're getting enough sleep?

Some people benefit from a power nap, or catnap, that lasts from five to twenty minutes. Note that if you sleep too long, you'll just wake up groggy and are likely to throw off your body rhythm. Meditation and breathing practices can give your body a sense of deep relaxation that may serve you better than a nap if you feel tired too much of the time.

Seven Tips to a Good Night's Sleep from the National Sleep Foundation

Want a better night's sleep? Try the following:

1. Consume less or no caffeine and avoid alcohol.
2. Drink less fluids before going to bed.
3. Avoid heavy meals close to bedtime.
4. Avoid nicotine.
5. Exercise regularly, but do so in the day-time, preferably after noon.
6. Try a relaxing routine, like soaking in a hot tub or bath before bedtime.
7. Establish a regular bedtime and wake time schedule.

Keep a sleep diary before and after you try these tips. If the quality of your sleep does not improve, share this diary with your doctor.

Dreaming

Have you ever awakened with a smile on your face, or a wildly beating heart and a feeling of fear, and not been sure if you were awake or still dreaming? It was once considered important to cultivate dream memory.

Everybody dreams, but there are many people who have no recollection of their dream state when they awaken. Ancient cultures had great respect for the powers of dreams to give us insight for growth and healing, but the tradition disappeared with the rise of religions that considered dream interpretation some kind of pagan hocus-pocus.

"We've rediscovered the ancient dream wisdom," says dream expert and author of *The Encyclopedia of Dreams,* Rosemary Ellen Guiley, "thanks to psychotherapy." Scientific studies on rapid eye movement sleep have verified that everyone has dreams. Guiley believes in their profound healing power. "Dreams do have meaning," she says. "They speak to us from the deepest levels of our being. They give us blunt and honest information about ourselves—they are the mirrors that reflect back to us how we think we're doing in life. They tell us how we feel about ourselves and our relationships ... what we really think about our jobs, abilities, and pursuits. They make us ponder spiritual questions."

To make a dream useful as a stress- and life-management tool, you may want to take action. Guiley says, "Dreams tell us what we need to change, and provide us with help in how to make those changes." That action can be as simple as acknowledging something about yourself, or changing an attitude, or even a direction in your life.

Rosemary Ellen Guiley's Dream Tips

Dreams are ephemeral and easily slip from memory. Immediately upon awakening, write or record everything you can recall; leave nothing out, no matter how bizarre or trivial. Every piece or symbol in a dream has meaning, and more subtle meanings reveal themselves upon reflection, meditation, or even over time. Colors have meaning also; they are associated with different states of consciousness, emotion, and physical health. Numbers may have meaning.

After some time, you may notice a pattern emerging in your dreams. These often revolve around unresolved issues or feelings. Your dream is calling your attention to these matters.

If you have trouble recalling your dreams, try these tips. Remember, it takes some time for the habit and ability to take hold.

- At bedtime, tell yourself you will remember your dreams.
- Remain in bed when you wake up and concentrate on the wisps of the dreams.
- Keep the dream journal as an invitation to your dreaming self to step forward.

61

Lucid dreaming is a technique that can help you remember your dreams in greater detail. It comes with practice and a kind of self-hypnosis before sleep in which you tell yourself you will remember every detail of your dreams. Jungian analyst Elizabeth Strahan, whose DreamWeavers company produces *The Language of Dreams* video series, says anyone can dream lucidly. "Invite your dreams to come, write them down. Dreams help us decipher and solve problems, give us insight into why we react to situations the way we do."

Once you've developed the habit of recording your dreams, you can find many books about dreams, mysticism, religion, and spirituality to help you interpret them. Guiley says your intuition will tell you when something clicks.

62

NUTRITION

"Scientific evidence continues to show that eating more fruits, vegetables, legumes, and whole grains, and selecting nonfat or low-fat dairy products and lean meats are important to good health," says Washington, D.C.–based Edee Hogan, R.D., spokesperson for the American Dietetic Association (ADA). A healthy diet is better able to help the body overcome the effects of stress.

There is evidence that B vitamins are linked to functions such as brainpower and stress; folic acid from leafy greens is recommended to prevent birth defects and may provide protection against Alzheimer's disease. Antioxidants such as vitamins C and E are being studied for their ability to neutralize polluting free radicals; to protect healthy cells, and fight off the lowered immune system response induced by stress; and possibly to slow the aging process. You can take supplements, but the best sources are natural goods.

"A high dietary intake of vitamin C may help reduce the effects of chronic stress by inhibiting the release of stress hormones," according to the Web site of former Surgeon General C. Everett Koop. These stress hormones can dampen the immune response, according to studies in rats. Dr. P. Samuel Campbell of the University of Alabama in Huntsville, who presented the findings at the 1999 meeting of the American Chemical Society, said this has implications for the prevention of stress-related illnesses in humans.

The essential fatty acids omega-3 and omega-6 are both important for health. When British researchers checked the levels of these fatty acids and examined the dietary intakes of people suffering from depression, they found a correlation between lower levels and intake, and higher depression symptoms. Omega-3s are found in flaxseed, pumpkin seeds, walnuts, and several coldwater fish. For omega-6s, use unsaturated vegetable oils such as safflower, soy, sunflower, flax, and walnut.

Low blood sugar can make you jumpy and irritable. Make sure you eat at least three balanced meals a day, with protein in each meal. Five small meals spaced evenly apart are even better, because small meals will help maintain your blood sugar level and avoid the hypoglycemic feeling of unease that comes with hunger. Eat mindfully—not on the run, not in the car, not standing in front of the refrigerator.

Weight control, or lack of it, is a common cause of stress. Increasing healthy nutrients along with an exercise program can

63

start you on the way to feeling better about the world, mentally and physically. There are a million weight-loss programs, most of which work only while you're on them. But if you dedicate yourself to being less stressed, you'll continue to make the healthy choices that will work in the long run.

Caffeine

Caffeine is a stimulant that generates a stress reaction in the body. There is evidence that too much of this substance—from coffee, tea, soft drinks, and even chocolate—can produce the symptoms of anxiety including increased heart rate and blood pressure, flutters and palpitations, and stomach upset. When stressed, it's a good idea to keep caffeine to a minimum, or eliminate it altogether.

You can see the effect caffeine has if you try to eliminate it for at least three weeks, but wean yourself gradually to avoid the side effects of caffeine withdrawal, such as headaches. In the long run, you will be more relaxed, sleep better, have more energy, and have less heartburn.

If the thought of a morning without your java is distressing, choose decaffeinated—it still contains some caffeine—and make it a ritual you mindfully enjoy. If you savor a really good cup, you can make do with less.

Water

You can survive in the wild for quite a while without food, but you wouldn't last very long without water, the number one "nutrient." It's been said that you need eight to ten glasses per day, but which *you* is that—the 250-pound linebacker working out preseason in 100-degree heat, the 95-pound coed who sits at a computer most of the time, or the average 150-pounder who works in an office and goes for a jog in the evening?

The Mayo Clinic in Rochester, Minnesota, says a good way to figure how much water you need is to divide your weight in half; this number in ounces is your recommended daily fluid intake. You also need to figure in exercise and other activities that make you sweat, as well as such dehydrating beverages as alcohol, coffee, and soda because they actually cause you to need more water.

Water is vital in the regulation of your body systems; every single part of your body depends on hydration to work properly. Water regulates temperature; removes waste; carries nutrients and oxygen to your cells; cushions joints; prevents constipation; removes some toxins; and helps to dissolve nutrients, vitamins, and minerals so your body can metabolize them well. The Mayo Clinic says adequate water intake can prevent kidney stones, and has been associated with a lower incidence of colon cancer.

Dehydration can make you function at below-normal levels and cloud your thinking. Mental confusion, ill health, or functioning below normal are all causes of stress. Drink water—to your health.

65

HERBOLOGY

Western medicine considers herbs useful when they are being applied to a particular condition. But in Chinese, Indian, Indonesian, and other cultures, herbs are used as tonics and teas to keep the energy flow or chi, to maintain the body's balance, and to keep the immune system in condition to fight off illness. An ancient Chinese catalog, *Shen Nung,* lists 365 plants used for healing.

By now you must have heard about "wonder herbs" such as Saint-John's-wort, SAMe, and kava. These herbs can be potent, and European studies have demonstrated some of their powers. The NIH has begun studies to see if their claims can be proven in U.S. clinical trials. Even though herbal preparations have been used in Chinese and Ayurvedic medicine for centuries, their purity and efficacy are just beginning to be evaluated according to U.S. standards. Doctors are only starting to be exposed to alternative therapies in medical schools.

You should always check with a physician before adding herbs to your daily routine. Some herbal compounds may raise blood pressure, affect hormone levels (particularly important if you are pregnant or have estrogen-related disorders or cancer), or cause irritability and allergic reactions.

In the May 1999 issue of *The AARP Bulletin* (published by the American Association of Retired Persons), an article titled "Be Smart, Beware: Herbs and Botanicals Can Help—but Can Also Harm" acknowledged that the National Toxicology Program of the Department of Health and Human Services and other U.S. institutions have begun to research the risks and benefits of several herbs, but "consumers need to do their homework to make sure they're not throwing their money away on useless products or, even worse, on products that may do more harm than good."

The Soothing Benefits of Herbal Teas

Coffeehouses may be replaced someday by a new kind of tea-house: the herbal emporium. With recipes based on Eastern traditions of herbal medicine, these custom-blended teas and elixirs are prescribed for mood, creativity, stress, and other conditions. Doctors of Chinese medicine—who should be consulted along with your regular physician if you want to treat a specific condition or are taking medication—are often on site at herb stores.

The Office of Dietary Supplements defines these substances as "products intended to supplement the diet that bears or contains one or more of the following dietary ingredients: a vitamin, mineral, amino acid, herb, or other botanical; or a dietary substance for use to supplement the diet by increasing the total dietary intake; or a concentrate, metabolite, constituent, extract, or combination of any ingredient described above; and intended for ingestion in the form of a capsule, powder, softgel, or gelcap, and not represented as a conventional food or as a sole item of a meal or the diet."

While the Office of Dietary Supplements does not yet regulate such supplements, promising studies are being done to determine their health-promoting and antiaging effects. Despite the long anecdotal history of such supplements, which describes their benefits, the Food and Drug Administration is not yet ready to endorse them unconditionally.

Cautions have been issued because overseas packagers do not always have production rules as stringent as those in the United States. Some problems have been reported with purity

67

and standardized doses of some herbal supplements. Major drug companies are jumping on the herbal bandwagon, so it probably won't be long before we know if claims about the benefits of herbs are scientifically sound.

Bags and herbal capsules are said by purists not to be as effective as whole leaves for brewing tea. "Fine tea is comparable to fresh, garden-grown fruits and vegetables," says John Armstrong, an "elixir tea master" at Elixir in West Hollywood, California. "It is bursting with flavor and nutrients, but impossible for commerce. . . . Those little flow-through body bags that populate most retail stores are filled with dead and dying remnants, pumped up with flavors, all too often artificial. What's more important, though, is that the essential oils, brimming with important healthful properties, dry out along with the tea."

68

Decaf Tea Trick

For people who want the benefits of green tea—it's been said to lower cholesterol, prevent heart disease, reduce the risks of some cancers, and ease stress—but who want to avoid the caffeine, the "elixir tea master" at Elixir in West Hollywood suggests an old Taoist trick: "Pour hot water over the leaves, let them soak for thirty seconds, then pour off this first round of water." This will carry away up to 80 percent of the caffeine, and still allow full flavor. Then, "Add a normal amount of hot water and steep as you normally would."

3

Relaxation Techniques

There are many effective ways to slow down and enjoy the proven mind/body/spirit benefits of mindful relaxation. No matter what your personality type, you are sure to find one technique to suit your spirit, your schedule, and your wallet.

THE RELAXATION RESPONSE

After three decades of pioneering stress research, Dr. Herbert Benson concludes, "All relaxation techniques evoke beneficial physiological effects." The original results of his still-ongoing research were published in a book titled *The Relaxation Response,* coauthored with Miriam Z. Klipper. This now-famous phenomenon developed when Benson discovered that the supposed benefits of transcendental meditation included lower blood pressure, heart rate, breathing rate, and metabolism. Benson, an academic cardiologist, decided to conduct clinical tests to see if this were true.

He found that relaxation can alleviate the symptoms of stress and stress-related illnesses. Benson's method, dazzling in its simplicity, is taught at the Mind/Body Medical Institute at Beth Israel Deaconess Center in Boston. Established in 1998, the center is "the first to give a home to the work of researching, teaching, and training about the mind/body connection." Now, many hospitals and clinics offer alternative therapies, doctors are beginning to incorporate spa treatments into their practices, and spas are offering medical consultation and wellness services.

70

Dr. Herbert Benson's Relaxation Routine
You can practice your own meditation for free at home, starting now.

Find a quiet environment.

Consciously relax your body's muscles.

Focus for ten to twenty minutes on the word *one,* or a brief prayer, or any simple word or phrase you like.*

Assume a positive attitude toward intrusive thoughts. (Don't worry about them, just refocus on your word or phrase.)

*"Love, peace, *and* relax *work for me."*

MEDITATION

Conventional Western allopathic medicine has come to recognize that we are more than the sum of our parts. We know now that the deliberate departure from the workday world is vital for well-being. Long an accepted part of Eastern culture, meditation at the very least can provide a respite from everyday pressures; at its most effective, it is downright healing.

Relax your thoughts and your body relaxes as well, stifling the bad stress hormones and inducing the good ones. The NIH's Office of Alternative Medicine is funding a variety of studies so doctors and universities can establish just which of these approaches yield proven benefits, and the results are exciting.

Dr. Carl Hammerschlag says, "Relaxation is meditation and meditation is relaxation. Either way you're going to alter your rhythm, suspend the ordinary, and tap into the extraordinary. You want to get into a different level of being that will put you in another place, where you can restore, replenish, regroup. Any way, all ways, are good, as long as you recognize the need to do it."

Once you've started searching, you'll find there are hundreds of meditation techniques. Religious gurus and Western corporate gurus have their followings. Community colleges, YMCAs and YMHAs, spas, and fitness clubs often offer meditation classes. Whatever the environment, you don't have to follow anyone's philosophy to reap the good from meditation. The general principles and results of the technique should be the same.

Meditation should ideally be practiced in a quiet environment; but once you have your technique down, you'll be able to

71

meditate anywhere. Still, overall results are best when noise and distractions are minimized. Low light or darkness can heighten the effects of meditation, even though your eyes should be closed. A moderate room temperature helps, as well as loose and comfortable clothing.

Meditation on Light and Breath

We sit comfortably, whether on a pillow or on a chair. Our hands rest in our laps, the right on top of the left, palms up and thumbs lightly touching. We keep the back straight without tightness, and the chin pulled in a little.

First we calm our minds. We feel the formless stream of air that comes and goes at the tip of the nose, letting thoughts and sounds go by without holding on to them.

Now we will meditate in order to experience mind and to gain a distance from our disturbing emotions. Only then can we really be useful to others.

Imagine a clear transparent light a foot and a half in front of your nose. While we breathe in, the light moves in a stream down through the center of our body. On its way, the clear light turns ever more red. Stopping briefly four fingers below the navel, the transparent light has become totally red. When we exhale naturally, the red light moves upward and becomes gradually more blue. A foot and a half in front of us, the blue transparent light again becomes clear and we inhale it once more. We hold this awareness without tension, while our breath comes and goes naturally.

If it is difficult to see the colors, we simply think them: clear light when we inhale, red light where the light stops below the navel, and blue when we exhale.

73

After a while, we may focus on the vibrations of our breath. While inhaling, we hear the syllable *om*. While holding the light below the navel, we hear a deep *ah*, and while exhaling we hear the vibration of *hung*.

We stay with this for as long as we like.

At the end of the meditation, the world appears fresh and new. We wish all the good that just happened may become limitless, radiate out to all beings everywhere, remove their suffering, and give them the only lasting joy, the realization of the nature of mind.

From Lama Ole Nydahl's *The Way Things Are: A Living Approach to Buddhism for Today's World* (Blue Dolphin, 1997). Used with permission.

Benson's relaxation response is a kind of meditation. You can choose to focus on a thought, word, or phrase, or on nothing at all. Some people concentrate on the "third eye"—the internal spot between the eyebrows—which some cultures believe is the window to the soul. Others try to evoke colors in their minds. Sounds are often focal points for meditation. These can be either external (e.g., New Age music, temple bells, or wind chimes) or internal (e.g., mantras or meditation words such as *om*.)

Whichever you choose, your mind may tend to wander and thoughts may intrude. Gently push them out of your consciousness and return to whatever you've chosen as your focal point.

Deepak Chopra says meditation is the first tool to prepare your mind and body for bigger and better things. At The Chopra Center for Well Being, meditation is the basis for "the path to wholeness," offered to help people with weight control, heart disease, cancer, and emotional problems.

74

BREATHING

One simple process that can greatly enhance your life is deep breathing. Indian yogis have long used deep breathing and meditation to put themselves into altered states that allow them to exist for months on little food, lie on a bed of nails, and perform other feats that don't seem humanly possible. These accomplishments—although in no way necessary for the layperson concerned with stress management—do remind us that we can have some control over our bodies, and our reactions to physical stressors don't have to be what one would expect.

"The process of breathing, of the fundamental movement of inspiration and expiration, is one of the great miracles of existence," according to Dennis Lewis, author of *The Tao of Natural Breathing*. "To breathe is to live. . . . Unfortunately, few of us breathe fully. We have lost the capability of 'natural breathing,' a capability that we had as babies and young children. Our chronic shallow breathing reduces the working capacity of our respiratory system to only about one-third of its potential, diminishes the exchange of gases and thus the production of energy in our cells, deprives us of the many healthful actions that breathing naturally would have on our inner organs, cuts us off from our own real feelings, and promotes disharmony and 'dis-ease' at every level."

"Breathing strongly influences mind, body, and moods," says Andrew Weil, M.D., author of *Eating Well for Optimum Health*. "By simply putting your attention on your breathing, without even doing anything to change it, you move in the direction of relaxation. Get into the habit of shifting your awareness to your breath whenever you find yourself dwelling on upsetting thoughts."

The Single Most Effective Relaxation Technique of Dr. Andrew Weil: Conscious Regulation of Breath

You can do this in any position, but I suggest you do it seated, with your back straight. (Keep the tip of your tongue against the roof of your mouth throughout the exercise.)

continued on next page

STRESS RELIEF & RELAXATION TECHNIQUES

1. Exhale completely through your mouth, making a whoosh sound.
2. Close your mouth and inhale quietly through your nose to a mental count of four.
3. Hold your breath for a count of seven.
4. Exhale completely through your mouth, making a whoosh sound to a count of eight.

This is one breath. Now inhale again and repeat the cycle three more times for a total of four breaths. Note that you always inhale quietly through your nose and exhale audibly through your mouth. Each exhalation takes twice as long as each inhalation. The absolute time you spend on each phase is not important; the ratio of 4:7:8 is important. If you have trouble holding your breath, speed the exercise up but keep to the ratio of 4:7:8 for the three phases. With practice you can slow it all down and get used to inhaling and exhaling more and more deeply.

This exercise is a natural tranquilizer for the nervous system. Unlike tranquilizing drugs, which are often effective when you first take them but lose their power over time, this exercise is subtle when you first try it but gains in power with repetition and practice. I would like you to do it at least twice a day. You cannot do it too frequently. Do not do more than four breaths at one time for the first month of practice. Later, if you wish, you can extend it to eight breaths. If you feel a little lightheaded when you first breathe this way, do not be concerned; it will pass.

You may also notice an immediate shift in consciousness after four of these breaths, a feeling of detachment or lightness or dreaminess, for example. That shift is desirable and will increase with repetition. It is a sign that you are affecting your involuntary nervous system and neutralizing stress. Once you develop this technique by practicing it every day, it will be a very useful tool that you will always have with you. Use it whenever anything upsetting happens, before you react. Use it whenever you are aware of internal tension. Use it to help you fall asleep. I cannot recommend this exercise too highly. Everyone can benefit from it.

People often ask me the reason for keeping the tongue in that position. Yoga philosophy describes two "nerve currents" in the human body, one positive, electric, and solar; the other negative, magnetic, and lunar. These begin and end at the tip of the tongue and the ridge behind the upper front teeth. Putting those structures in contact is supposed to complete a circuit, keeping the energy of the breath within instead of letting it dissipate. I don't know if there is any correlation between these ideas and Western concepts of physiology, but since yogis have been doing this exercise for thousands of years, it seems worth following their instruction exactly.

77

www.meditate

Jim Malloy started meditating when he was a teenager in the '60s just because it was the thing to do. "It was just like the doors of perception were flung open," he says. His energy level shot up, but it went deeper than that. "I started getting all this incredible insight about the meaning of life and what we are here for." Now a teacher of meditation, part of what he's here for is to help others reduce stress and enhance life's pleasures. Try a meditation break from his www.meditationcenter.com.

Inner Light Meditation

This meditation is meant to direct the experience of your calm, unbounded Inner Spirit, tap into your spiritual energy, increase the flow of fuel to your brain, and open your sixth chakra—the Inner Eye—for clear insight, inner vision, relaxation, and stress reduction. It uses the light that is already within you as an object of focus. It's fairly simple but quite powerful and potentially very deep.

Sit comfortably with your eyes closed.

Look at the inner screen that fills the space behind your brow.

There will be particles, images, or patterns of light on this screen. Gently focus your attention on the light.

Don't try to create or interpret things. Don't attempt to focus clearly. Simply look at the light with relaxed attention.

If you feel as though your consciousness is shifting, or you are slipping into a dreamlike state, allow it to happen. Whatever you experience is okay.

If you find you have drifted off into your thoughts, simply bring your attention back to the light on your inner screen.

79

Diaphragmatic Breathing

This is a technique often used before and after a yoga session. It serves as a transition to and from regular activity, and is something anyone can practice at any time or in any place. You can do this breathing from the diaphragm, or "belly breathing," for as little as one minute to reap the benefits. If you practice it daily for ten to twenty minutes, your body and mind will thank you.

All you have to do is breathe deeply, slowly, and evenly, allowing yourself to fill up with air all the way from your belly to your shoulders. Once you've learned the practice lying down, you'll be able to use it whenever you need a literal and figurative shot of oxygen—at your desk, at a stoplight, or in line at the grocery store.

Lie down on the floor or bed with your arms comfortably at your sides. If you have back problems, bend your knees or put a towel or bolster under them to ease the pressure off your lower back. Relax all your muscles and feel yourself sink into the floor. While you inhale slowly, watch your stomach rise like a balloon. Continue the breath so you can feel your lungs fill with air slowly all the way to the top. As you exhale, feel the air leave your lungs first, and continue to exhale until your stomach "balloon" goes down. Continue to exhale as you tighten your abdominal muscles. Pull them in and toward the floor or bed, and try to visualize them touching the bottom of your spine. Then begin the process again, watching your stomach and chest rise and fill with air from bottom to top. Then empty the breath from top to bottom.

Keep all your muscles relaxed. When you first practice, you might find you've tensed your arms and shoulders or legs and buttocks. Just consciously observe your body and let go when you become aware of any tension. Keep letting go, breathing deeply, letting your abdomen and chest fill and empty.

Yoga Breathing

There are lots of breathing techniques from yoga used to clear the body and mind. Breathing deeply while holding one nostril closed, then the other; breathing in one nostril and out the other; breathing in deeply, then releasing in a short but full burst while making a sound like "hah"—all these methods serve to energize and relax you by "oxygen therapy."

Deep Breathing

There are many deep-breathing techniques you can use to relax or refresh yourself during the day.

Here's an exercise: Keeping the tip of your tongue against the roof of your mouth, breathe in slowly through your nose, then exhale with an audible expression of air. You will notice all your muscles relaxing with the exhalation. Do this ten times.

Breath Visualization

Close your eyes, breathe in slowly, and imagine the air coming in as a white light. See it fill your body, with each breath swirling in and spreading down and around. Imagine it flowing into your internal organs, from the lungs into the shoulders and arms, and then into your fingertips. Continue until you feel filled with the light.

81

Any number of breathing routines are offered in classes and books, but all follow the same principle. Focus on the breath, consciously relax your muscles with each exhalation, and you'll have a mini-vacation any time you need it.

www.relax

Yoga has been adapted for "mouse potatoes." Julie Lusk, M.Ed., L.P.C., regional director for four hospital-based holistic centers in Cincinnati, Ohio, presents a series of more than one hundred stretches she refers to as "hacker yoga" in her book *Desktop Yoga*. It's a good thing to put on your list of "favorite places" to use as a break. When you're sluggish or stiff from

continued on next page

too many hours at the computer, practice this yoga-based stretching routine provided by Lusk, who teaches and writes about it as well on www.relaxationstation.com.

Neck Stretch
Sit up straight and allow your shoulders to relax. Let your right ear move toward your right shoulder. Only move it as far as is comfortable without force. Take a few full, deep breaths. Just as your muscles begin to tire, take a breath in and bring your head back up to the center.

Next, let your left ear slowly move toward your left shoulder and take a few more breaths. Then, bring your head to center on an inhalation. It is common for one side to feel more limber than the other side.

Repeat moving your head from side to side several times. While doing this, imagine all the stress and strain that's held around your neck releasing and letting go.

Next, let your chin glide down to your chest and take a few breaths. Remember to let it go as far as is comfortable without stress or strain. When ready, bring your head up to center.

Do not move your head backward. It puts too much stress on that area of your neck.

Energy Stretch
Place both feet flat on the floor and let your arms hang to your sides. As you breathe in slowly, begin raising your arms straight out in front of you until they are shoulder level. Still breathing in, bring your arms out to both sides and then raise them over your head.

Breathe out as you lower your arms back down to your sides. Continue for several deep, diaphragmatic breaths.

83

The trick here is to raise your arms during the time it takes to breathe in and to lower your arms during the time it takes to breathe out. Practice makes perfect.

Palming
Rub your hands together with your palms and fingers touching. Keep doing it so that you feel some heat and energy being generated. Next, rest your elbows on your desk. Cup your hands and gently place them over closed eyes. Let the warmth and darkness soothe your eyes. Take several long and easy breaths as you imagine the tiredness being released with each exhalation and energy and vitality returning with each inhalation.

STRESS RELIEF & RELAXATION TECHNIQUES

PROGRESSIVE
MUSCLE RELAXATION

Alternately tensing and relaxing all the muscles in your body one by one is a technique called "Progressive Deep Muscle Relaxation," developed by Edmond Jacobson, M.D.

Sit or lie down, close your eyes, and take a few deep breaths. Begin to tighten your muscles one at a time or in groups. You can start at the top of your head and work down, or begin with your toes and work up. Squeeze and tighten each muscle or group for five seconds, release quickly, and relax them for thirty seconds. For example, tighten your fingers hard into fists, then release and relax them. You can do hands-only, or as muscle groups with your arms also tightened hard and released at the same time. Another example would be to squeeze your abdominal muscles tightly against your spine, then release. Or squinch up your face: Purse your lips, squeeze your eyes shut, tighten your jaw, then let them all go at once.

This technique is often used at the end of aerobics and other fitness classes. Once you get the hang of it, you can do it quickly at any time to release tension during the day. It's very effective at bedtime, when you're already under the covers and ready to release the tension of the day. It will help you drift off to a relaxed sleep.

Think Relax

Once you've mastered the technique of relaxing your muscles and breathing deeply, you can try the "think relax" method any time you feel yourself tensing up—during a frustrating business meeting, in the middle of an argument, at the grocery store behind a person with twenty-five items in the express check-out line.

You can start with the part of your body that normally is the first place you tense up; it's different for everyone: forehead, jaw, shoulders, stomach, back. If it's your head, for example, start by thinking, "Scalp, relax." You'll naturally release the tension as it starts to build up. Continue: "Brow, relax; jaws, relax; tongue, throat, neck, relax." Try it now; you'll feel it, and it will get better once you've practiced some of the techniques above.

85

Focus

Focusing, or centering, is the basis for all relaxation therapies. While you go through your normal routines, you often react involuntarily to the stressors you encounter. When you determine to focus on something as simple as your breathing or to concentrate on a mantra, stressful thoughts are pushed away and your mind can quiet, your body can relax. When you have let go all the tension, your spirit can go free, and you can tap into your higher self.

Progressive Relaxation from IDEA, The Health & Fitness Source

First, find a quiet, peaceful place where you are not likely to be interrupted. Set a timer for twenty minutes and ensure you will remain undisturbed for that time. Put on soothing, gentle music—or choose silence—and start the timer. Lie on a firm, cushioned surface or thick blanket with your arms open and palms up. You can choose from several positions, including the following:

- Lie with your legs straight out but relaxed.
- Rest your thighs over a bolster, with your knees bent and feet relaxing on the floor.
- Rest your lower legs on a chair, with your knees bent at a right angle.

Or try other positions, just as long as you're comfortable.

Method

Lie in your preferred position and take a few deep breaths, focusing on the exhalations. Feel yourself becoming heavier and heavier.

Surrender your body weight to gravity. Give yourself mental permission to relax.

Imagine your feet becoming relaxed. . . . Feel them sinking into the floor . . . followed by the legs . . . hips . . . lower back . . . abdomen . . . chest . . . shoulders . . . arms . . . hands . . . fingers . . . head . . . and all your face muscles.

As you exhale, relax each body part, allowing each part to feel very heavy. Let the music carry you into a pleasant daydream. Allow yourself to be with whatever thoughts come up, or drift into a deep sleep.

Ending the Relaxation
When the timer rings, stretch your arms overhead. Take long, slow, deep breaths; hug your knees to your chest, and roll over onto your side. Stay there a minute or so before sitting up sideways, bringing yourself back into the reality of the moment. You should feel alert but calm when you go about your business.

Variations
Play a relaxation audiotape instead of music. A soothing, hypnotic voice can help you surrender more easily, especially if you are very tense.

87

A Simple, Powerful Breathing Practice

Though this practice can be done any time of the day or night, it is especially beneficial in the morning, just before you get out of bed. It will help detoxify your inner organs and center and energize you for the day ahead. Over a period of time, it will begin to transform your breathing, making it deeper and more harmonious.

1. Lying on your back with your feet flat on the bed and your knees bent (pointing upward), follow your breathing for a minute or two. See if you can sense which parts of your body your breathing touches.

2. Now rub your hands together until they are warm.

3. Put your hands (one on top of the other) on your belly, and watch how your breathing responds.

4. You may notice how your belly wants to expand as you inhale and retract as you exhale. Let this happen, but do not try to force it.

5. If your belly seems tight, rub your hands together again until they are warm, and then massage your belly for a couple of minutes, especially right around the outside edge of your belly button. Notice how your belly begins to soften and relax.

6. Now put your hands on your belly again and just watch how this influences your breath. Do not try to do anything. Simply watch and enjoy as your belly begins to come to life, expanding as you inhale and retracting as you exhale.

7. When you are ready to stop, sense your entire abdominal area, noting any special sensations of warmth or energy. Let these sensations spread into all the cells of your belly, all the way back to your spine.

This simple practice can have many benefits, especially if you do it on a regular basis. Remember that you can try this at any time of the day or night, sitting, standing, lying down—whatever is most practical for you. It is also an excellent practice to work with whenever you are anxious or tense; it will help relax you and center your energy.

89

From Dennis Lewis's *The Tao of Natural Breathing* (Mountain Wind Publishing, 1997). www.authentic-breathing.com. Used with permission.

BIOFEEDBACK

Alpha waves are brain waves that indicate a deep state of relaxation. These are measured by electrical hookups placed on one's head, body, or hands and fingers and connected to a biofeedback machine. Biofeedback is based on the theory that you can learn to control some physiological responses that used to be considered involuntary. The benefits come when you've learned to recognize the signals that accompany pain and distress, and to use your awareness along with techniques such as breathing or meditation to recover a state of relaxation. It has been used by doctors and physical therapists to treat chronic pain such as that from migraine headaches and lower back problems, as well as urinary incontinence and other conditions. Psychiatrists and psychologists use it to help tense, anxious patients relax.

Electronic sensors feed data on temperature, respiration pulse, skin moisture, and muscle tension to an audio or video monitor as your body reacts to a variety of stimuli, such as sound, pictures, or thoughts. By studying the monitor, people can learn to recognize their feelings of tension and to give themselves cues that will initiate relaxation.

Once you learn the technique with a professional, you'll recognize those indicators of stress and alter your reactions to them. Proponents claim you can learn to relax specific muscles; reduce your heart rate, respiration, and blood pressure; change your body temperature; improve digestion; and even alter your brain's electrical activity.

According to Bette Runck, a staff writer for the Division of Communication and Education at the NIH, "The word *biofeedback* was coined in the late 1960s to describe laboratory procedures then being used to train experimental research subjects to alter brain activity, blood pressure, heart rate, and other bodily functions that normally are not controlled voluntarily." Now that we know that we can alter these functions and create relaxing countereffects to stressors, Runck says it means people who use biofeedback are aware that "they must accept much of the responsibility for maintaining their own health."

If you want to try biofeedback, consult only a health-care professional who has been trained to use it.

VISUALIZATION

Imagine yourself on the shore of the clearest, bluest sea. The sun warms your face, the breeze wafts gently over your body. Palm trees sway, and sea birds soar over the gentle waves. Lying on a fluffy towel against the hot sand, you are relaxed and at peace. This is an example of the visualization technique. Carl Jung called it "active imagination."

In addition to its use for relaxation, visualization can also promote healing. Cancer patients may imagine Pac-Man-like figures traveling through their bloodstreams to "eat up" all the cancer cells. Migraine sufferers can imagine soothing waves breaking the muscle tension in their pounding heads.

You can use this technique anyplace, any time you feel the need to get away. Just find a quiet room and a few minutes to close your eyes.

GUIDED IMAGERY

If you've ever been given a pep talk, you already know what guided imagery is: visualization with external help. Relaxation tapes often feature speakers with soothing voices helping to guide

91

you to a place of security and comfort. Guided imagery is sometimes also a combination of guided meditation, visualization, and affirmation. The guide describes the environment and suggests relaxation, and the guided lets go and goes along for the ride.

Part of the reason guided imagery works for relaxation is that your attention is directed to imagining and feeling a place of pleasure and security. That takes your attention off the factors that have been contributing to your stress. Alona Zisfain, Ph.D., uses the technique for her psychotherapy clients who are too distraught to settle down at the beginning of a session: "When people have suffered physical or emotional injury on the job, or are very anxious or depressed, I find a good way to help them relax is the use of a technique such as guided imagery.

"By focusing on slow, deep breathing, and taking them to an imaginary place that appeals to them—imagining the sense of color, smell, sound—the process is helpful in diverting their focus away from the stressful event. Once the practice is mastered, clients can use it at their own convenience outside the sessions."

"Imagery is the natural language of the unconscious mind," say Martin L. Rossman, M.D., and David E. Bresler, Ph.D., who established the Academy for Guided Imagery (AGI) in Mill Valley, California. "A guide in guided imagery helps connect what clients see in their images." AGI has developed its own Interactive Guided Imagery process to help people "connect with the deeper resources available to them at cognitive, affective, and somatic levels."

"Imagery is not just wishful thinking," say Rossman and Bresler. "A growing body of medical research shows that imagery has a powerful influence on every major control system of the

Typical First-Time Session of Interactive Guided Imagery

In what is called the "foresight aspect" of the process, the client and guide discuss their goals in using Interactive Guided Imagery (IGI)—relaxation, symptom relief, insight, problem solving, conflict resolution, etc. The guide assesses the appropriateness of using IGI; if it is deemed right, they move into the "imagery aspect."

The client usually begins the imagery portion of the session by getting comfortable and relaxing. The guide might talk the clients through a basic relaxation exercise, or they might simply relax by themselves.

From a relaxed state, the client might simply be asked to allow an image to form of the area of concern, illness, or interest. As an image forms, the guide would facilitate an interaction between the client and the image to help clarify and offer insights into the situation.

After interfacing with the image for an appropriate period of time, the guide would gradually assist the client back to ordinary awareness, then together they "debrief" the session. The session lasts fifty to ninety minutes.

93

Source: Academy for Guided Imagery.

body—stimulating vital functions like heart rate, blood pressure, local blood flow, wound healing, even immune system function. Imagery can be helpful in as much as 90 percent of all the problems people bring to their doctors. . . . "

Rossman's book *Healing Yourself* is the basis for a program he teaches to patients and health professionals. He says the program works because it encourages participants to relax deeply; promote self-healing; focus within to become aware of and understand their symptoms and needs; and act on what they have learned.

AFFIRMATIONS

94

We've all had words lodge in our subconscious minds after we've heard them repeatedly. All too often, we remember mostly the negatives: "You're stupid," "You're ugly," "You're incompetent." Fortunately, positive statements can work the same way, and replace negative messages. This mind-trick can lead the way to personal growth, increased self-confidence, and lessened stress. These positive statements are called "affirmations."

If you have a good awareness of who you are and what goals you have, you can custom-tailor them. You can set aside a few minutes to think them, say them out loud, or write them down. Some people do their affirmations while brushing their teeth or shaving, looking right into the mirror and giving themselves a visualization pep talk.

For example, on a given day you could say to yourself, "I am creative" or "I am going to be calm today." If outside situations are threatening your sense of self, it might be a good time for "I am a good person" and "I deserve to take time for myself."

HYPNOSIS/SELF-HYPNOSIS

Hypnosis and hypnotic suggestion have been a part of healing practices for thousands of years. Shamans and medicine men often healed with the power of suggestion. Greek healing temples used variations of the technique. Modern medicine has demonstrated its value by validating the existence of a placebo effect: If the mind believes a substance has the power to heal, it will have a healing effect on the body, even if the substance was in fact innocuous.

Hypnosis as we know it arose in the eighteenth century with Franz Anton Mesmer, an Austrian physician who treated a range of illnesses, psychological and psychophysiological, with what he termed "magnetic healing." Sigmund Freud used hypnotherapy for a time. Today, hypnosis is used effectively for substance abuse, pain control, and phobias. It is being used in concert with other kinds of relaxation and medical therapies for diabetes, allergies, and asthma.

Like affirmations, self-hypnosis can help you let go of self-defeating thoughts and replace them with images to enhance your self-esteem, strengthen your resolve, and clarify your goals in love, work, and relationships.

A self-hypnosis relaxation tape may guide you through deep breathing and muscle-relaxing techniques, then deliver positive messages such as these from the Furthermore Foundation's *Relax into Excellence*: "I am letting go and putting out of my life all tiredness and lethargy, and I am now replacing these negative feelings with the feelings of constructive, enhancing, fulfilling, productive energy. . . . I am now putting out of my life all disease: mental, emotional, physical, and spiritual, and I am now replacing

95

these diseases with complete mental, emotional, physical, and spiritual health." Try saying these aloud.

Arthur Hastings, of the Institute of Transpersonal Psychology in Palo Alto, California, uses relaxation techniques and self-hypnosis to help people to release and clear their minds. "Most people in this current work and business climate need ways to step out of their envelope of stressful demands, to loosen their bodies, and soothe their minds," he says.

"Self-hypnosis can be used to reduce physical tension and mental stress through self-instructions to relax muscles and nerves, and to calm the mind," Hastings says. This technique can overlap with other stress reducers like progressive muscle relaxation and visualization. "With eyes closed, you mentally tell your body to relax, one part at a time, and consciously release tension and tightness as you go. In that relaxed state, instructions are given to the self to become calm, to step aside from the worries and pressures, and to feel a sense of tranquillity." With practice, the mind and body begin to follow these instructions. You can learn to do this through books, tapes, and qualified hypnotherapists.

NATURE TAPES

Audio- and videotapes that offer the restful sounds of nature are the next best thing to getting out to the beach, desert, mountains, or forest. For years, CBS's *Sunday Morning* show has set aside a short nature scene with no sound but the birds or wind, and it has remained a popular feature. Even city people enjoy stopping for a moment of quiet respite from urban noise.

Environment tapes can be used for a quick "vacation" into a rainstorm, down to the ocean, or deep into the jungle. Use the calming sounds as a background to practice deep breathing, progressive muscle relaxation, or just being mindfully in the moment. (See also the music therapy section in chapter 5.)

AROMATHERAPY

The olfactory sense has a direct connection to the brain and can have immediate psychological effects. These can evoke emotional reactions: Chocolate chip cookies may remind you of home; a whiff of cologne brings back memories of a first love; newly mowed grass may put you back into elementary school when afternoons were free for tossing a ball around the yard.

97

Aromatherapy is the art and science of using aromatic plant essences specifically for improved mood enhancement, relaxation, and health. Practitioners say these essential oils have the ability to help stimulate your immune system to heal and handle stress.

Aromatherapy is an integral part of many native cultures. Essential oils have been used in medicines, teas, potions, and lotions; as burning incense; and as ritual bath preparations. Eastern and Western religions use aromatherapy: joss sticks in China, incense at Catholic mass, havdalah after the Jewish sabbath. Chinese and Indian medicine describe therapeutic and spiritual uses of plants and herbs. Frankincense, myrrh, and cedarwood were used to embalm the pharaohs. "During the great plague in seventeenth-century England," says aromatherapist Geraldine

Howard, "it was noticed that people who worked with plants and herbs—especially the lavender sellers—seemed to have some immunity. Everybody started to carry posies of sweet-smelling flowers and herbs to ward off the disease." It wasn't until the eighteenth century, Howard says, that industrialization offering chemical alternatives led to the waning use of aromatic medicines.

When French chemist René-Maurice Gattefosse burned his hand in a laboratory accident, he coated it with lavender essence on the assumption that lavender had antiseptic properties. He recorded that the "healing began the next day." This spurred him to investigate many plant extracts; resulted in his 1928 book, *Aromatherapie*; and led to the birth of modern aromatherapy.

98

Clinical studies continue to investigate the effects of aromatherapy to see if it can be classified as more science than art. Researchers at Memorial Sloan-Kettering Cancer Center in New York did a study showing that fragrance can reduce distress and anxiety experienced during magnetic resonance imaging (MRI), a procedure often required to diagnose life-threatening illnesses. Sharon Manne, Ph.D., and William Redd, Ph.D., found that people exposed to an appealing fragrance while undergoing the procedure had 63 percent less anxiety than a control group who were not.

Essential oils are highly concentrated aromatic essences of plants. Some scientists say they are part of the survival and immune systems of the plants, or possibly the by-products of plant metabolism. In their pure form, essential oils are not to be applied or ingested directly. They should be kept away from direct sunlight and heat, as they are volatile and flammable.

Practitioners say essential oils affect the nervous system as well as muscular tension, and should be used in massages, facials, and hydrotherapy baths, as well as in candles and scent diffusers. Oils can be chosen for quieting or stimulating, decongesting, and detoxifying.

How to Use Essential Oils

These oils are most often diluted with pure vegetable carrier oils, such as almond, grapeseed, or jojoba. They can be diluted in water for hydrotherapy. Because essential oils have not been tested scientifically for the treatment of illness and disease, it's best to consider aromatherapy primarily for relaxation and cosmetic purposes, unless you are seeing a physician who specializes in alternative therapies. Even for cosmetic applications, the use of essential oils depends not only on their purity but also on the aromatherapist's knowledge to blend them for specific applications and personal conditions.

"In the home," says Judith Jackson, author of *The Magic of Well-Being* and producer of Judith Jackson Aromatherapy products, "aromatherapy can be used for the face, for the body, and for bathing and room fragrance. It's even nice to combine all four uses, to have a complete experience. The effect is dictated by what kinds of essential oils you use. If you're feeling tired, rosemary and lemon are a good pick-me-up. If you're feeling nervous, a little lavender and chamomile. If you're just in need of balancing, sandalwood is wonderful."

When purchasing aromatherapy products, look for natural, pure essences. An inexpensive candle may give off the aroma you like, but aromatherapists say the relaxing and soothing effects

99

are not the same if they contain synthetic compounds. No studies have been done on the topical application of synthetic fragrances for health. On his Web site, Dr. Andrew Weil advises "some aromatherapy candles emit such hazardous pollutants as acetone, benzene, lead, and soot. Since these harmful substances can impair the quality of indoor air, you have to be cautious about the aromatherapy candles you purchase.

"The National Candle Association suggests you protect yourself by buying beeswax candles, which are cleaner and safer than those made with paraffin wax (the fumes of which have caused kidney and bladder tumors in laboratory animals). Also watch the wick," Weil cautions. "A wick that gets too long while a candle is burning may be releasing soot into the air (always keep wicks trimmed to ¼ to ½ inch).

"As much as possible," Weil adds, "you should also make sure that candles are scented with natural essential oils rather than synthetic fragrances. This isn't always easy since candlemakers aren't required to list ingredients on their labels." Instead of candles to create an aromatic environment, you could try evaporating the oils in a diffuser, vaporizer, or incense burner; or dilute them with water and disperse via atomizer.

Products Derived from Essential Oils

Essential oils blended for different conditions, including muscle soreness, relaxation, and anxiety, are used in massage and hydrotherapy. Bath salts blended with essential oils for a long soak in the tub are a great relaxer. Spas offer a variety of facial and body treatments that incorporate aromatherapy.

How to Use Aromatherapy in Everyday Life

It is easy to improve the mood of any room with the addition of a diffuser. By simply adding a few drops of essential oil to a diffuser dish filled with water and lighting a candle underneath, you can fill a room with scent, which can be surprisingly effective in changing your mood. Try peppermint in the bathroom for a refreshing morning eye-opener, or marjoram or lavender by your bedside to help you sleep at night. Lemon, basil, and rosemary are mind-stimulating and good for the office. Try a blend of these for increased concentration.

You can add essential oils to your skin and hair products. Oil of orange, ylang-ylang, and rose are good for shampoos. Chamomile and tea tree are soothing for the skin.

Source: *Auroma News*, Volume 1 (Fall 1988). Used with permission.

101

Aromatherapy products are everywhere, and almost every beauty company is offering a selection. Aveda, for example, was at the forefront of using therapeutic aromatherapy in its products, and has dedicated itself as a company to protecting the planet by using pure essences. Aromatherapy products are becoming inventive; for example, Aroma Dough comes in a stress-relieving Play-Doh-like ball imbued with essential oils, so you can squeeze the stress away in traffic or at your desk. There are tiny diffusers made of pottery that are meant to hang from the rearview mirror to scent the air in your car. You can dab some essential oil on a cloth and wipe it across your dashboard. Carry a vial in your purse or pocket, replacing the posies of old. Jurlique makes a Travel Blend of essential oils in an atomizer specifically for traveling, as do other companies.

However the scents work, aromatherapy is a reminder to stop, take a sweet-smelling breath, and relax.

Flower Remedies

Similar to aromatherapy is the flower remedy. Flowers picked in full bloom are soaked in spring water, and the blossoms are discarded. The essence that remains is mixed with brandy or other spirits, then diluted with additional water into therapeutic doses. The prepared essences are taken by drops under the tongue, in water for sipping, on the skin, or added to a bath.

The flower remedy most familiar today was developed in the late 1920s and early 1930s by an English homeopathic physician named Edward Bach. He was ahead of his time in thinking that illness could come from underlying emotional problems. Bach also believed that there was a connection between specific negative personality traits and certain illnesses.

Bach used thirty-eight different wildflower essences to treat physical conditions and moods or attitudes. Research continued after his death in 1936, and many more kinds of flowers are in use for Bach Flower Remedies today. There has been no scientific research to prove these flower remedies cure disease,

Relaxing Blend

For Massage

7 drops lavender

7 drops pettigrain

7 drops chamomile

1½ ounces vegetable oil
     (soy, jojoba, sunflower, or grapeseed)

Mix the drops of pure lavender, pettigrain, and chamomile essential oils with the vegetable oil, called the "carrier oil." You may vary the amounts of each essential oil to suit your own preference.

For Diffuser

When using an aromatherapy diffuser, you do not have to use the carrier oil. Simply place the essential oils directly onto the diffuser. Or, sprinkle the blend in a bowl of boiling water and leave it in the room for a relaxing atmosphere.

For Sleep

Sprinkle the blend of essential oils onto a pillow or sachet.

Source: Aromatherapy Associates. Used with permission.

103

but, anecdotally, they do seem to ease stress and tension, and control certain types of chronic pain.

HYDROTHERAPY

Hydrotherapy is the therapeutic use of water for healing. Warm water induces relaxation, and soaking in your own bathtub is the easiest, handiest hydrotherapy of all. In some circumstances, hot and cold compresses are considered forms of hydrotherapy. Swimming is therapeutic. A whirlpool or Jacuzzi, sauna, and steam room all can provide the benefits of muscle relaxation.

Spas, or sites with healing waters, were visited by soldiers and saints throughout history. Some attribute the name to a famous quote by the emperor Nero: "Sanitas per Aquas," or "health by water." If you belong to a gym or fitness facility, try to use hydrotherapy to wind down and relax the muscles you've been flexing throughout your workday and workout.

There are wonderful technological improvements on the old whirlpool to be found in clinics and spas. Special tubs can be adjusted to simulate lymphatic or athletic massage. Mineral salts and essential oils can be added to create an aromatherapy session. The bubbles can be adjusted to make you feel as if you're sitting gently in a glass of champagne; a more vigorous setting can effect a big circulation boost. Some of these devices are computer programmable for a variety of sensations.

Used in European and American spas as water-massage techniques, the Scotch Hose and Vichy Shower work out the kinks and improve circulation. The Scotch Hose is delivered in a shower stall; multiple needle-spray shower heads and high-pressure water hoses, alternating hot and cold temperatures, are directed at pressure-point areas of the body by a therapist. The Vichy Shower looks like a human car wash: A long bar with multiple shower heads rains down from above while the client lies on a special massage table. It usually follows a body treatment.

Hydrotherapy has been used at European and Asian spas and clinics for centuries. Doctors there prescribe it as part of a total health-care protocol. In those locations, mineral salts, seawater, or planktons and muds are often used topically in massage or added to the water in a pool or tub. Overseas, studies have demonstrated the healing powers of such preparations, but in the United States they have come under the jurisdiction of the cosmetics industry rather than the Food and Drug Administration.

105

Kerstin Florian, who has studied mineral hydrotherapy for many years and produces Spa Kur products, says that this practice is an important part of the European philosophy that "total well-being is comprised of good nutritional habits, an ongoing exercise program, peace of mind, and a treatment regimen for the body." Florian considers hydrotherapy to be "a natural medicine that affects the whole body. Warm water has a sedating effect on the nerves and muscles, which helps to reduce stress. I believe in the restorative and regenerative properties of mineral waters through centuries of noted benefit," she says.

Soaking in warm water relaxes your muscles, increases your circulation to eliminate toxins, and relieves physical tension. It often allows your mind to loosen up as well, giving you the chance to reflect and gain new perspective to neutralize your stressors.

**Indulgence: Make Your Own
Scented Bath Salts**
A scented bath is an instant retreat, the perfect evening relaxant for you or a friend.

Total time: 10 minutes

Total cost: $10

Materials needed: 1 cup of Epsom salts, 2 tablespoons of baking soda, your favorite essential oil, and an airtight jar or bottle

Directions: Mix together Epsom salts, baking soda, and 20 drops of essential oil. Pour into jar, and close. Tie a ribbon and a nice note around the jar for a wonderful gift.

Source: Christine Dimmick, The Good Home Company, www.thriveonline.com. Used with permission.

COLOR THERAPY

Using color therapies for healing and relaxation is based on the Eastern concept of chakras. *Chakra* means "wheel" in Sanskrit, and refers to seven wheels of energy that revolve or rotate around chakra points of the body. They begin at the base of your spine and end at the top of your head; located at the front or back, they work through the body. Each chakra is represented by a color. When each energy center is healthy and in balance, the colors are pure and bright.

When imbalance, underdevelopment, poor physical condition, illness, disease, or stress block the energies, the life force is slowed and the chakras reflect these conditions. Practitioners believe that when the body is in a state of imbalance, so are the emotions and thought processes; if you react to unpleasant emotions by blocking your feelings, you stop much of your energy flow.

Clairvoyants say they can see these chakras, viewing them as wheels, or multipetaled flowers of color when they are open. Each one has its own characteristic speed and vibration, slowest in the root chakra at the bottom and fastest in the crown chakra at the top. Rebalancing them with various therapies is supposed to restore a feeling of calm and well-being.

Some practitioners use crystals and gemstones in color therapy, which they say work on what science calls the piezo-electric effect, that is, electricity or electric polarity created by pressure in a crystalline substance such as quartz.

107

LIGHT THERAPY

Seasonal affective disorder is a condition in which symptoms of depression affect people who haven't been exposed to enough sunlight. It usually occurs in the winter, particularly in places with extremes of bad weather and in parts of the world where daylight hours are few. Studies have found that full-spectrum fluorescent light produces the same color spectrum as natural sunlight and can be effective in neutralizing depressive symptoms and enhancing feelings of well-being.

Chakras

First: Root chakra

Color: Red

Location: At the base of the spine at the tail-bone in back, and the pubic bone in front; governs hips, legs, lower back, and sexual organs*

Function: Survival mechanism; controls fight-or-flight response; need for security and safety

Crystals: Garnet, ruby, coral, jasper

108

Second: Spleen or belly chakra

Color: Orange

Location: Just above the navel; governs sense of self-worth, ability to relate to others; governs kidney, bladder, large intestines, and sexual organs*

Function: Center of emotions; sexuality, creativity

Crystals: Carnelian, agate, Madeira citrine

Interesting Mars/Venus note: Some say because a man's sex organs are located mostly in the first chakra, male sexual energy is experienced primarily as physical. A woman's sex organs are mainly found in the second chakra, so female sexuality is primarily experienced as emotional. Both of these chakras are associated with sexual energy.

Third: Solar plexus chakra

Color: Yellow or gold

Location: Just above waist, behind stomach

Function: Center of will, personal power, ego, passion, impulse, anger, and psychic development; mental versus physical control; governs stomach, liver, gallbladder, pancreas, and small intestine

Crystals: Yellow citrine, light smoky quartz, yellow diamond, tiger eye

109

Fourth: Heart chakra

Color: Green or pink

Location: Just above breastbone

Function: Love, compassion, emotions; governs heart, lungs, circulatory system, shoulders, and upper back

Crystals: Emerald, green malachite, peridot, green calcite, jade, watermelon tourmaline, rose quartz

continued on next page

Fifth: Throat chakra

Color: Light blue or turquoise

Location: Center of throat at V in collarbone

Function: Center of communications in thought, speech, and writing; inner hearing; ability to change and heal; governs throat, neck, teeth, ears, and thyroid

Crystals: Turquoise, aquamarine, blue topaz, blue malachite, aqua aura quartz, celestite, blue tourmaline

Sixth: Third eye chakra

Color: Indigo blue

Location: Center of the brow

Function: Inner sight, psychic ability, intuition, link to higher consciousness; governs eyes, brain, and the lymphatic and endocrine systems

Crystals: amethyst, violet tourmaline, sapphire, lapis lazuli, sodalite

Seventh: Crown chakra

Color: White or violet

Location: Top of the head or just above

Function: Spiritual life force, universal consciousness, spirituality, inner wisdom; said to be where "silver cord" connects aura to body

Crystals: Quartz crystal, white diamond, opal, calcite

Some lore says there is an eighth chakra clear of color: the Transpersonal Point, Heavenly Chi, or Soul Star, said to carry a person's reasons to incarnate into this lifetime. Believers say if you place your palm several inches above the center of your head, you will feel a tingling sensation where the eighth chakra is.

111

The so-called atypical depressive symptoms such as carbohydrate cravings, prolonged sleep, weight gain, and increased appetite were shown to improve in a study by the Department of Psychiatry at the University of Helsinki, Finland. Subjects trained in a gym with more than average light were compared with those who exercised under normal light and to a group of people in supervised relaxation classes. The researchers concluded that even healthy people can improve mood and health-related quality of life during wintertime by exposure to bright light.

Typically, light therapy involves exposing people to special lamps that are ten to twenty times brighter than average indoor lighting. Studies in the 1998 *Archives of General Psychiatry* concluded that this light therapy is most effective when administered first thing in the morning. If you are feeling sad, try going for a walk before you start the rest of your day's activities.

Light therapy is sometimes available at spas and wellness clinics, as well as psychiatric treatment centers. The Spa Grande at Grand Wailea Hawaii, for example, offers it as a treatment to "increase energy level, restore relaxation response, improve sleep patterns, enhance concentration, balance appetite, and diminish jet lag." They sometimes combine it with music therapy for focused attention and more relaxing effects.

LABYRINTH

"We are overstimulated and exhausted spiritually in our ever-changing, competitive world," says Georgina Lofty, a licensed marriage, family, and child therapist in Long Beach, California, who hosts the SacredWalk Web site, and presents labyrinth walks and workshops. "The labyrinth is being rediscovered as a walking meditation/prayer tool to provide people with a means of experiencing peace in these hectic times."

An intricate pathway full of twists and turns, a labyrinth is a metaphor for life. Constructed in a circle, it is an ancient symbol for wholeness. Labyrinths are often confused with mazes, but mazes take unexpected twists and turns, and have many dead ends. A labyrinth, however, has only one path, circuitously one way in and out. Labyrinths are usually designed with seven, eleven, or twelve circuits. With each turn you move 180 degrees; changing directions is said to shift your awareness from right brain to left brain. This is one reason why labyrinth devotees say the practice can alter your state of consciousness and balance your chakras.

The path is the journey to the center and back, and it represents your own life journey—sometimes meandering but always purposeful. When you lose your way in life and need to rethink your purpose, a labyrinth is a good place to walk for prayer and meditation.

113

There is no right or wrong way to walk a labyrinth. "Expectations inhibit what the experience may hold," says Lofty. "The most important thing is to open your heart and begin a spiritual path. Trust that only in this moment of time, with one step, one breath at a time, life and all the glory of the Divine unfolds."

Labyrinths can be found all over the world. The most famous in the Western world is built into the floor of Chartres Cathedral, near Paris, France. Built around A.D. 1200, the labyrinth was used in prayer or as a symbolic pilgrimage to the Holy Land. As a gesture of repentance, some worshipers would follow the path on their knees. At Grace Cathedral in San Francisco, California, a replica of the Chartres labyrinth welcomes visitors amid an Interfaith Meditation Garden. Rev. Lauren Artress at Grace Cathedral has been instrumental in the labyrinth revival with her book *Walking a Sacred Path*.

The Hopi people are said to have called the labyrinth the symbol for Mother Earth. Labyrinths were part of many Native American traditions, as well as those of the Greeks, Celtics, and Mayans. Whether constructed permanently in stone, tile inlay, and paint or of temporary materials such as sand, cornmeal, painted canvas, and natural vegetation, labyrinths are looked upon as sacred places for personal introspection and growth.

At the Ojai Valley Inn & Spa in Ojai, California, the labyrinth is set under a tree near the herb garden. The Golden Door in Escondido, California, has one, as do several retreats, spas, and resorts; the labyrinth is indeed becoming a modern-day meditative tool. Most labyrinths are set apart, in location and in spirit, giving you the opportunity to remove yourself from your routine for meditation and introspection.

A finger labyrinth is a small reproduction of a larger one, usually printed on paper. Some say taking a break to let your fingers trace and retrace the paths can be a stress-relieving mini-meditation.

114

GADGETS AND GIZMOS

Flotation Tanks

Floating is a relaxation therapy based on the principles of Reduced Environmental Stimulation Therapy. Research has demonstrated that deep relaxation and clarified thinking are accomplished when outside stimuli are removed.

In 1954, John C. Lilly, M.D., a pioneer in brain and behavioral research, experimented with the idea of limiting extrasensory brain stimulation. With his first isolation environment, he thought he would demonstrate that the brain would simply "go to sleep" without its usual exposure to input. He was surprised to find the opposite: Without visual, acoustic, tactile, and temperature stimuli, Lilly found that the brain functioned at a higher-than-normal level. Using a flotation tank removed the effects of gravity, as well.

Lilly found that "the gravitational force on the body coupled with noise, light, and temperature ... utilized approximately 90 percent of the neural activity in the brain. Once one's mind is freed from the physical environment by this technique, one has the whole range of the human mind available to one's imagination; one's thinking capacity is at maximum."

One unexpected benefit of floating is the profound state of relaxation engendered by the stimulus-free environment. Popular in the 1960s, the Samadhi or flotation tank is making a comeback under brand names such as the Oasis.

115

Betar Bed

Looking like a bed made for outer space, the Betar bed is a steel construction placed in a room filled with the scent of lavender. A multispeaker system plays uniquely chosen music while you meditate in the illusion of floating on a bed of sound. One of sixteen in the world can be found at Sanibel Harbour Resort & Spa in Fort Myers, Florida.

Light/Sound Machines

A variety of light machines use white or colored bulbs to foster an environment for meditation and relaxation techniques. Several sound machines are on the market as well, offering white noise to enhance sleep, or a variety of nature sounds and music for an ambience conducive to relaxation. Some, like the Mind Gear Light/Sound machines, are combinations of both.

"Flickering lights and controlled rhythmic tones stimulate brain waves to lower, more relaxed frequencies," says Philip Brotman, M.D., a biofeedback practitioner and product distributor. "Some mind machines produce binaural signal sounds, feeding one continuous tone to the right ear and a slightly different tone to the left ear, producing a beat frequency in the brain."

Alpha-Stim

116

The Alpha-Stim is an electromedical device used to treat stress-related disorders, insomnia, and chronic pain. It is based on cranial electrotherapy stimulation studies, which grew out of previous therapies known as "electrosleep" and "neuroelectric" therapy. The Alpha-Stim uses "unique wave forms of tiny electrical currents similar to those found naturally in the body to reestablish bioelectrical control systems," says its developer, Daniel Kirsch, Ph.D., D.A.A.P.M., F.A.I.S.

When your body regains a healthy homeostasis, or balance, your brain works better and your immune system works properly. Raymond B. Smith, Ph.D., Alpha-Stim's director of science, says, "There is nothing quite like cranial electrotherapy stimulation to help people find relief from anxiety, depression, and insomnia. Because it stimulates the brain to produce neurotransmitters, it increases endorphin production, and enhances cognitive function. This has been useful in treating alcoholics, whose cognitive and immune functions have been out of homeostasis for prolonged periods."

The currents are delivered through ear-clip electrodes. Sessions are self-administered and usually recommended for twenty minutes, every other day. "Most patients report a warm, relaxed feeling of well-being, which is caused by smoothing brain waves. For pain patients, results can be immediate," says Kirsch.

Alpha-Stim is available over the counter in Canada, Europe, Asia, and other countries, but only by prescription in the United States.

4

Bodywork

Touch is a powerful stress reliever, and somatics, or body-work, comes in many forms. Massage therapies, energy therapies, hydrotherapies, and psychological therapies that include working with the body are physically therapeutic techniques that are effective precisely because of the power of touch. A mother's gentle stroke on the brow can ease a fever, a paternal arm around the shoulder can keep a Little Leaguer on two feet after a hapless slide, and a friend or lover can stop your tears with a hug.

Because of the human need to connect, it's very beneficial to be touched and massaged. Physically, massage works the tension out of the muscles, increases range of motion, and improves circulation, thus promoting relaxation and a sense of well-being. Eastern-style massage practitioners say it frees blockage in the energy flow, or chi, of the body. Proponents say those blockages can lead to ill health, and freeing them can keep the body in tune.

Massage Information

- Choose a trained and accredited massage professional.
- Your therapy should take place in a warm, quiet, comfortable environment, with a special massage table.
- Sometimes soft music or nature tapes will be playing. If a particular musical selection interferes with your comfort, do not hesitate to ask that it be changed.
- Discuss your physical conditions, medications, concerns, and goals with your therapist beforehand.
- Vein problems, cardiac conditions, high blood pressure, skin conditions, infectious diseases, and pregnancy can contraindicate or alter some massage procedures.
- Generally, a client will be nude for the therapy. The therapist should leave the room so that you can disrobe and set yourself under the sheet. If being nude makes you uncomfortable, you may choose to wear underwear or a swimsuit.
- You should be properly draped with a sheet or towel throughout your therapy. Only the area being worked on will be exposed.
- Make yourself comfortable. The therapist will gently move you or tell you what you need to do.

- Speak up immediately if any body position or massage stroke is painful or uncomfortable.
- Feel free to ask questions at any time during the session.
- You may feel so relaxed that you fall asleep during your therapy; this is OK.
- If you practice deep breathing or other relaxation techniques during your massage, you'll reap twice the benefits.
- The average massage session lasts about an hour.

121

There is definitely a mind–body component of physical therapy; though it is hard to quantify, many people report a greater sense of peace and well-being after treatment. When your body is relaxed and relieved of tension, your mind can be free to explore the health of your body and spirit, creativity is sparked, introspection is heightened, and self-improvement is inspired.

The American Massage Therapy Association reports that "people are getting more massages, and that therapeutic massage is becoming more mainstream, appealing to everyone from young adults to seniors." It also reports that men and women are getting massages in comparable numbers, "mostly to relax, relieve aches and pains, and help reduce stress." The association credits the rise in massage popularity to the baby boomers' interest in preventive medical care.

The Touch Research Institute at the University of Miami has led the way in studying touch and its applications in science and medicine. Infants who were touched while adults smiled and cooed at them displayed more eye contact and had better responses than those who were smiled and cooed at without touch. Preterm infants who received massage gained more weight, slept better, and were more active than those who were left alone.

Elderly volunteers who performed infant massages reported lessened anxiety and depression, lowered pulse rate, decreased cortisol levels (high levels of which adversely affect the immune system), increased self-esteem, and a better lifestyle (e.g., fewer doctor visits, more social contact). These effects were stronger for giving than receiving massage, suggesting that there are dual benefits to this practice.

Massage has been shown to have positive effects on people with premenstrual syndrome, high blood pressure, asthma, attention deficit hyperactivity disorder, autism, anorexia, back pain, bulimia, carpal tunnel syndrome, sleep disorders, some psychiatric disorders, and posttraumatic stress disorder. It has alleviated depression and anxiety for people with chronic fatigue and cystic fibrosis, teenage mothers, and others. Massage therapy administered during labor decreases anxiety, pain, length of labor, and the need for medication.

At the University of Medicine and Dentistry of New Jersey–New Jersey Medical School, students who were massaged before an exam showed a marked decrease in anxiety and respiratory rates, as well as a significant increase in white blood cells, suggesting enhanced immune system activity. At the James Cancer Hospital and Research Institute in Columbus, Ohio, cancer patients reported less pain and anxiety after massage.

It's no wonder that massage therapy relieves everyday stress, promotes relaxation, and affirms the mind–body connection. In a 1998 *Newsweek* article, Tiffany Field, Ph.D., founder of the Touch Research Institute, said she "puts massage in the same category with proper diet and exercise as something that helps maintain overall health."

"Massage not only feels wonderful," says the American Massage Therapy Association. "Research has proven it has myriad health benefits."

123

MASSAGE THERAPIES

Acupressure

Pressing on energy centers, or acupoints, is based on the Asian practice of acupuncture. When the energy points, which lie between energy pathways called meridians, become blocked or congested, pain, discomfort, frustration, irritability, lowered immune system function, and spiritual confusion may result. In acupressure, gentle but deep finger pressure is applied to the energy points to release the free flow of chi. It has been effective in relieving chronic pain, insomnia, nausea, fatigue, muscle tension, stress, and anxiety. Releasing the blocked energy allows your body and mind to relax.

Chi Nei Tsang

Chi Nei Tsang (CNT) practitioners work deeply into the belly. It is too simple to call it a massage therapy. CNT practitioner David Lewis says, "CNT is an educational process using massage, acupressure, and guided breathing to help people clear negative or unhealthy energies, as well as various toxins, from their internal organs, tissues, and bones, and to transform and recycle these energies to promote physical, emotional, and spiritual health. CNT also uses meditation techniques involving internal awareness of colors and sounds to aid in the detoxification and transformation process."

CranioSacral Therapy

This is a gentle method of evaluating and enhancing head and spinal cord functions, and thus, says John E. Upledger, D.O., O.M.M., "is effective for a wide range of medical problems associated with pain and dysfunction." Upledger developed the technique based on the theories of osteopath William Sutherland, O.D. This massage, Upledger says, relieves "energy cysts" or constricted areas in the brain that hold emotional trauma.

"The craniosacral system consists of the membranes and cerebrospinal fluid that surround and protect the brain and spinal cord," says Upledger. "It extends from the bones of the skull, face, and mouth—which make up the cranium—down to the sacrum, or tailbone area. Since this system influences the development and function of the brain and spinal cord, an imbalance or dysfunction in the craniosacral system could cause sensory, motor, or neurological disabilities."

CranioSacral Therapy is used to locate and solve problems throughout the body. Upledger says that "it encourages your own natural healing mechanisms to improve the functioning of the central nervous system, dissipate the negative effects of stress, and enhance your health and resistance to disease." An outgrowth, or expansion, of this method is the mind–body retraining technique known as SomatoEmotional Release Therapy, designed to rid the mind and body of the residual effects of trauma.

Esalen Massage

The Esalen Institute pioneered the human potential movement of the 1960s, and it was one of the first retreats where Eastern philosophy met Western. The alternative lifestyle retreat on the California coast is known as a place for self-exploration, meditation, and education. Mindfulness is part of all its activities, including massage. Both therapist and client participate in Esalen massage. It combines long, lengthening strokes with gentle rocking and stretching, passive joint movement, deep muscle and cranial work, and pressure-point technique. Esalen calls it "touching with purpose, to relieve muscle pain, increase body awareness, or bring equilibrium to a life in crisis."

Lymphatic Drainage

Also called manual lymphatic drainage, the premise of this massage therapy is that the perfect flow of lymph promotes elimination of toxins for a healthy immune system, and that by opening

125

up the lymphatic system, the body will attain homeostasis, or balanced body chemistry. Similar to Swedish massage, it was developed by Dr. Emil Vodder and Estrid Vodder, and is also called Vodder lymph drainage.

Myotherapy

You have but to take your shoes off for myotherapy. Developed by media fitness pioneer Bonnie Prudden, it is based on the theory that when "trigger points"—places of hyperirritability in the muscles or fascia—are met with physical or emotional stress, a muscle can spasm, causing extreme pain. When the therapist presses on the offending trigger point and "reeducates" the surrounding muscles to return to a normal position, the body can resume its healthy alignment. Myotherapy also improves circulation and energy, enhancing posture and athletic performance and decreasing insomnia.

Neuromuscular Therapy

Neuromuscular therapy is based on the idea that when you are stressed and in pain, your body goes out of whack because body parts will compensate for something amiss in one place by balancing it in another. It is often used for cases of chronic pain caused by injury or tension. When tissues are constricted, blood and nutrients can't flow in and toxins can't flow out. A neuromuscular therapist will assess these factors, along with posture, energy levels, and other physical considerations, and then counsel you in nutrition and stress reduction along with mechanical realignment using trigger-point therapy.

Reflexology

Practiced for millennia in Oriental medicine and as part of the Ayurvedic tradition, reflexology is based on the belief that zones on the feet, hands, and ears correspond to organs and body parts, and manipulation will cause them to reflex, or be stimulated, for healing, improved circulation, and a return to balance. The therapy is applied by specific pressure on zones of the feet by the technician's thumb and fingers. Practitioners say it increases circulation, which encourages removal of toxins, stimulates the immune system, improves blood pressure, and encourages healing. It can be a deeply relaxing experience.

Reflexology is relatively inexpensive and is today offered at many spas, hospitals, and alternative health-care centers. Research into its positive benefits continues worldwide. There are cards and even socks printed with the zones clearly delineated so you and a partner can try it at home, but it is a good idea to have at least one professional session so you know how it should feel.

127

Shiatsu

You don't have to disrobe for this massage. Traditionally administered while the client is lying on a floor mat, shiatsu is a Japanese technique in which finger pressure is applied to specific points, which are believed to free the energy (chi) pathways of the body. This helps to reduce fatigue and sluggishness, and to stimulate circulation, nerves, muscles, and energy level. It is sometimes called Zen acupressure, Zen shiatsu, or simply Zen massage.

Spinal Release Therapy

Also known as spinal integration, this massage therapy technique is based on a philosophy similar to neuromuscular therapy: Your body has a center of gravity, which is supported by your muscles and the tissues of the lumbar area. When you are injured, muscles contract and distort, causing pain and misalignment. Spinal release therapy uses a technique of rubbing out the kinks, encouraging the muscles to correct distortions of the central nervous system and to restore the body's center of gravity.

Sports Massage

Also called athletic massage and performance massage, this therapy was developed in Russia to help athletes perform at maximum capacity. But you don't have to be an athlete to enjoy its benefits: increased circulation, improved flexibility, muscle relaxation, injury prevention, and balancing of body and mind.

Stone Therapy

A new trend in massage treatment, this therapy uses natural stones as massage tools. Smooth stones, usually basalt, are placed under and on top of the body, along chakra (energy) points. Different sizes and colors are used, and they are applied hot and cold. The therapist may hold a stone while applying massage strokes. Sometimes stones are placed between the fingers and toes to stretch them and increase circulation in the limbs.

The popularity of this unique treatment has given rise to many variations: La Stone is a version created by Mary Nelson-Hannigan that is fast gaining popularity at all types of spas. Some therapists gather their own stones and feel a spiritual connection to the healing service; in their hands this massage takes on a deeper dimension.

Swedish

The most commonly performed massage therapy and the most well known, Swedish is a classic gentle, relaxing massage. Devised by Henri Peter Long in the early 1880s in Sweden, this technique uses oil to reduce the friction of five specific movements (long strokes, kneading, tapping, rolling, and vibration) and is administered to ease muscle aches, relieve tension, improve circulation, and promote relaxation.

Thai Massage

Nuat phaen boran thai means "the old Thai way of healing with the hands" and was practiced by Buddhist monks and nuns as they spent hours sitting in meditation. They probably learned it from Indian yogis spreading the Buddhist word from Indonesia approximately 2,500 years ago. According to therapist Yosel Tarnofsky, this "powerful hands-on therapy is neither Thai nor massage. It is meditation and movement for two people. Because I believe the word *massage* limits the definition of this incredible yoga medicine, I usually refer to it as Thai/Yoga Body Therapy," says Tarnofsky. "The focus is not merely physical but to balance the mental, emotional, and spiritual aspects of the individual as well. It appears to be a combination of acupressure shiatsu, hatha yoga, and reflexology, with some aspects of massage." Also known as Nuat Bo Ram, Nuat Thai was adapted by Anthony James, Ph.D., based on the original technique. It is said to relieve stress and enhance a sense of well-being, in addition to the benefits gained from all massage therapies.

Trager

Also called Trager psychophysical integration, this physical therapy technique was developed by Milton Trager, M.D., for relaxation, stress release, and sensory repatterning of the mind. It uses applied pressure and gentle rocking motions for body realignment. Practitioners say it helps release your mental hold on your muscles.

Trauma Release Therapy

A ten-step protocol of interactive techniques to rebalance the head, face, and body, trauma release therapy was developed by Karl Nishimura, D.D.S., M.S., for relieving temporomandibular joint dysfunction (TMJ) and jaw and tooth-grinding disorders. TMJ is often a symptom of chronic stress and results in jaw pain, headache, earaches, and thus more stress. Trauma release therapy is also used for craniofacial orthopedics and to reduce the pain and inflammation from acute stressors such as wounds, accidents, and falls; and chronic stressors such as fibromyalgia, tendinitis, arthritis, and bursitis.

130

Trigger-Point Massage

Also called pressure-point or tender-point massage, a forerunner to neuromuscular therapy, "trigger point" was coined by Janet G. Travell, M.D. This technique uses finger or thumb pressure on specific points of muscle and connective tissue that trigger pain in an effort to reduce spasms and muscle sensitivity and correct referred pain.

Watsu

Developed by former Beat poet Harold Dull, Watsu is a combination of shiatsu massage and hydrotherapy. Working in a special pool with water near body temperature and chest high, the Watsu giver stretches and swirls you in a kind of water dance. This technique leads to a deep state of relaxation and increased range of body motion that Watsu receivers say takes massage therapy to another dimension; they often describe it as "going back to the womb." Because the water provides buoyancy, it allows people of all sizes and physical conditions to experience stretching and healing from muscles constricted because of physical and mental trauma. Watsu is used for physical rehabilitation as well as stress management.

131

Watsu Variations

Therapies inspired by Dull's Watsu students include Aqua Soma and Wasser Tanzen, which use underwater music and flotation devices. Waterbalancing is a similar system offered by the inAqua

Institut in Germany, with underwater dolphin sounds and videos. Liquid Sound is another variation, performed at special saline pools in Germany and Austria with dolphin and whale songs and colored lights.

Watsu: Freeing the Body in Water

To know what Watsu is, it must be experienced, if not in real water, at least in the imagination. This can be done because elements of Watsu have counterparts in everybody's experience.

Begin with the way you relax when you lie back in warm water. Add how it feels to be slowly stretched. Imagine how, in an element that removes pressure from joints and radiates warmth into muscle, you feel each stretch all the way through your body.

Add to the pleasure of being floated and stretched what you feel in the best bodywork when the tension in your neck is sensitively released, when your shoulder is rotated and freed, when just the right point is held. Imagine how that is amplified when, instead of weighing heavily on a table or floor, your body is free to move.

Add your most nurturing memory of someone holding, supporting you, just being with you, not trying to do anything to you, holding you so lightly you feel your own lightness as you sink and rise to the rhythm of your breath.

Combine all of the above and there is still something to add—Watsu's flow. Watsu interweaves movement and stillness. It has a beginning and an end. And it is endless. Its lessons in letting go into the flow whatever comes up (and a lot does come up) can be carried into your everyday life. Watsu's feeling of still being centered at the end when you're no longer being held can rebond you to that part of your being that is one with everything.

Source: *Watsu: Freeing the Body in Water* by Harold Dull. Used with permission.

Zero Balancing

"A hands-on body/mind system representing the integration of Eastern views of energy with Western views of science" is the way the Zero Balancing Association describes this modality. Fritz Frederick Smith, M.D., developed Zero Balancing after his studies of osteopathy, medicine, chiropractic, and acupuncture joined with his introduction to Swami Muktananda. It is a gentle touching and pressing technique with a deeply relaxing effect, based on the theory that we hold emotion and injury in our bones as well as our muscles. "When that blocked energy is cleared," says practitioner Deborah Brigham, of Calabasas, California, "it can be transformational—as focusing and calming as it is healing and relaxing."

MIND–BODY RETRAINING

There are a number of therapies based on the integration of mind, body, and spirit. Predicated on the interrelationship of mechanical injury or dysfunction and emotional trauma and chronic patterns, they involve massage, physical manipulation of muscles and fascia, and retraining with conscious awareness.

Alexander Technique

The Alexander technique is a therapy designed to reeducate the mind and body. Australian Shakespearean actor Frederick Matthias Alexander developed it in the 1890s after doctors were unable to help him overcome his vocal problems and fatigue on the stage.

Alexander believed that discomfort and pain are a result of habitual tightening of the muscles, of which we may not even be aware. This throws off our sense of balance and we compensate in inefficient ways, after a time accepting the imbalances as normal. Alexander's technique makes you aware of the way you move and educates you to use just the appropriate motion, tension, and energy for each movement.

It's a method that "helps a person discover a new balance in the body by releasing unnecessary tension," says therapist Robert Rickover. "It can be applied to sitting, lying down, standing, walking, lifting, and other daily activities." Once you've become aware of a physical problem and learned how to solve it with correct movement, the technique can be preventive against future imbalance.

Changing the way you think about moving to relieve stress patterns requires a series of these treatments. "To change ingrained body movements and stances," say Andrew S. Levine, L.M.T., and Valerie J. Levine, Ph.D., authors of *The Bodywork and Massage Sourcebook*, "you have to exert mental energy in the forms of paying attention, engaging in detailed self-examination, and visualizing yourself making the corrective actions."

Aston Therapeutics

135

This was developed by Judith Aston, a former professor of dance and movement and a pioneer in the field of body mechanics. Aston Therapeutics is a method of assessing and analyzing the body as a unique ecological system. It analyzes the body at rest and in motion to find alternatives to stressful movement habits.

Feldenkrais

Another theory about how unhealthy physical habits can be retrained by Awareness Through Movement, the Feldenkrais Method was developed by Moshe Feldenkrais, who was born in Russia in the early 1900s. He moved to England, and liked to participate in vigorous activities such as judo and soccer. When a serious injury left him unable to walk, his doctors didn't even think surgery would help.

Feldenkrais reeducated his body to move in ways that would ease his knee pain. Teaching himself to walk again, he eventually realized that the way we move can create physical pain and mental stress that is in turn rooted in childhood development. "The Feldenkrais Method is not something that is done to you," according to the Levines. "Rather, it is a learning experience. It is a system, rather than a treatment."

The therapist guides you through a sequence of movements and you focus on how you perform them and on how to relax and release. As you follow verbal instructions to first isolate body parts—for example, using your arm as a paintbrush—and then to coordinate multiple movements with your breathing, you can let go of destructive habits and develop awareness, flexibility, and enhanced coordination. Learning how to move properly through this awareness helps prevent future distress and misalignment. The many artists who pursue this therapy believe it also enhances creativity.

Hakomi

Hakomi is a cutting-edge form of body-centered therapy in which the sensations, impulses, tensions, and movements that occur in a therapy session take on as much importance as what is verbalized in the session. Ron Kurtz named this therapy from an ancient Hopi word that means "How do you stand in relation to these many realms?"

"It integrates the wisdom of Taoism, Buddhism, and somatic intelligence with traditional psychotherapeutic methods," says Kurtz.

Certified Hakomi therapist Barbara Shaw, M.A., says Hakomi's goal is to consciously access the ingrained belief systems that can cause our bodies to be in distress without our knowing why and how. "If you believe the world isn't safe, you will not take risks. If you believe you are not a good person, you may not be able to have intimate relationships," Shaw says. Hakomi helps people become aware that certain beliefs may have been appropriate for emotional and/or physical survival, but time has passed and those defenses are no longer necessary or beneficial. "Once you become aware, you can learn compassion and acceptance of yourself and others, and realize you have a choice in how you react to the world." Certified Hakomi therapists learn how to observe the "subtle things happening to a client on the edge of consciousness that aren't noticed until you slow down," says Shaw.

137

Guiding clients through body awareness, mindfulness, and breathing techniques in a safe, nurturing environment is as much an art as a skill. "Sometimes one or two sessions are enough to remove physical symptoms of stress," says Shaw. "Then, there are people who want to clean up everything, open up the boundaries of self-knowledge and creativity."

Hellerwork

Joseph Heller considers this mind–body work, which he developed in 1979 after having specialized in Rolfing, a process for personal growth. Hellerwork is based on the theory that the usual massage modalities don't work in the long run. Poor postures and old movement patterns will return unless one is trained to release the thoughts and emotions that originally caused the dysfunction.

"This is a good therapy for people whose heads are ahead of their bodies," says Heller. "They've talked things out intellectually, but their bodies remain the same. Some things are engraved in the flesh and Hellerwork can work them out. As opposed to psychotherapy, you don't have to know what caused the trauma, but you do have to be willing to let it go."

Hellerwork's holistic approach includes a series of sessions using breathing technique, deep-tissue bodywork, and discussion between the therapist and client about particular body parts. "Movement reeducation and dialoguing are very important parts of Hellerwork. They allow the person to maintain the benefits of the work, and to improve upon it," says Heller. Different modalities work better for different people. "Hellerwork is good to counter the wear and tear of aging, the ravages of stress, and the remnants of past physical trauma."

138

Process Acupressure

"Process" refers to the free-flowing way this hands-on mind–body work session unfolds, as opposed to a structured psychotherapy modality, according to Aminah Raheem, Ph.D. She has developed this unique therapy during which "soul consciousness is evoked to come forth" and guide the session. The acupressure massage procedures are based on Rolfing, Zero Balancing, and a synthesis of the many therapies Raheem has studied. She says when this protocol is used, "Whatever is going on for the client automatically comes to the surface. You don't have to probe and push for it. It's just there. . . . All I have to do is just start opening the energy and their own being presents it. . . .The most essential purpose of process acupressure is to expose and empower people's souls, so that they can then fulfill the purpose they are meant to fulfill in this life, by processing the obstacles, even when they are traumatic and frightening."

Rolfing

Developed by Ida P. Rolf so she could overcome a family illness, this therapy was originally called structural integration. Sometimes very painful, Rolfing involves deep muscular manipulation and movement education that proponents say correct the effects of past trauma and injury. Clients report profound emotional release along with muscular tension. Usually given over ten sessions, the therapy is said to enable better stress management and coping ability.

Rosen Method

The Rosen Method is based on the theory that we hold memories in our muscles. Marion Rosen, P.T., left Nazi Germany, where she had studied relaxation techniques, and completed her physical therapy degree at the Mayo Clinic before settling in California. By the mid-1970s, Rosen had developed this nonjudgmental touch, talk, and assessment modality by which people become aware of the stored feelings and memories that affect our muscle tension.

ENERGY THERAPIES

Can electromagnetic forces affect you? Are there powers not yet measured that influence your health and well-being? Can a therapist "touch you" without touching you?

To date, scientific research on subtle energies has been confusing, but historic medical traditions have accepted the interrelationship between all the forces of the earth for thousands of years. "Nonlocal phenomena such as prayer and healing intention have a venerable history, and, like any human activity, represent a valid area of scientific inquiry," says the Institute of Noetic Sciences.

The Institute has been at the forefront of research and education in consciousness and human potential since *Apollo 14* astronaut Edgar Mitchell came back from his mission filled with the conviction that "the beautiful blue world to which he was returning is part of a living system, harmonious and whole, and that we all participate . . . in a universe of consciousness."

Trained as an engineer and scientist, Captain Mitchell never abandoned "the world of rationality and physical precision," but once he had witnessed the incredible scientific achievement of space exploration, he felt "the uncharted territory of the human mind was the next frontier." He established the Institute for this purpose—*noetic* coming from the Greek *nous*, or "ways of knowing."

According to the Institute, "Experiments in recent years suggest with increasing persuasion that the influence of human healing intention can operate across both spatial and temporal boundaries, lending support to claims by healers throughout the world who believe that they can restore the health of their patients in the absence of physical or mental contact. What we need now is a focused program which involves both qualitative research and formal experimentation."

Energy Healing/Biofield Therapeutics

Basketball Hall-of-Famer Rick Barry played some hard games but managed to come back physically from every one of them. One day, after his lauded playing career had come to an end, he tried to pick up a rock in his garden and strained his back. Then he hurt his knee. The pains just never seemed to diminish, and a friend referred him to an energy healer named Gloria Kaye, Ph.D. Trained to be a psychotherapist, Kaye discovered she could use her natural gift to sense or feel energy imbalances in her patients.

"Energy work just seems to relax people," Kaye says. Redirecting the energy allows the body to go into a state in which it can find its natural balance and heal itself. After a brief discussion and visual assessment of a client, she observes the imbalances in the face and shoulders, and the symmetry of the entire body. "I try to determine which areas of the body are compensating for injury or trauma," she writes in her book *Is There a Healer in the House?* Biomechanics and balance are interrelated: "When you're straightened out, your chemistry will change."

"Nothing is in isolation," she says. "If the hand has been injured, chances are that the arm and shoulder have been affected. This creates an even greater imbalance. I frequently tend to the injured area after I have made corrections elsewhere in the body. I have found that if the energy is flowing freely through the body, the affected area will be more prepared to receive the healing energy. Energy healing works quickly, because the energy is moving on a cellular level to put the body back into balance," Kaye says. "The energy just seems to go where it is needed."

Kaye says this healing has to do with the transmission of a subtle energy. She feels she is not really the healer but rather a conduit for the energy, clearing the blockages that occur from physical and emotional trauma, directing it back to its rightful pattern of flow. She became aware of her "gift" (she prefers that to the word *power*) when she was a girl. Friends just seemed to heal from severe pain and injury when she was nearby and feeling concern and sympathy.

142

"I work intuitively, and allow my hands to lead me. Many times my hands will seek areas that appear to be unrelated to the complaint for which a client came," says Kaye. For example, what seems to be a strain in the back turns out to be arthritis in the elbow.

Rick Barry wasn't really a believer, but he saw Kaye only a few times, and now his physical problems rarely interfere with his golf game. He has come to realize there is more to physical fitness than previously thought, and has since worked with a company that produces fitness and healing products that use magnets as therapy to redirect energy flow.

Biofield therapeutics, also called the "laying on of hands," is a time-honored form of medicine. "The underlying rationales cluster around two views," according to the Office of Alternative Medicine's (OAM) *Fields of Practice: Manual Healing*. "First, that the healing force comes from a source other than the practitioner—God, the cosmos, or another supernatural entity—and second, that a human biofield directed, modified, or amplified in some way by the practitioner is the operative mechanism."

Sessions last from twenty minutes to an hour; a series of sessions is needed to treat some disorders. "There is a consensus among practitioners that the biofield permeates the physical body and extends outward for several inches. The extension of the external biofeed depends on the person's emotional state and health," says the OAM, which reports that about fifty thousand practitioners provide eighteen million sessions in the United States annually. Most often, the therapies are Healing Touch, therapeutic touch, and shen therapy. The OAM adds there is "no generally accepted theory that accounts for the effect of these therapies." Non-believers say these therapies work through a placebo effect. The NIH has funded further studies.

143

Reiki

An ancient form of Japanese healing, *reiki* translates as "universal life energy." In the late 1800s, Dr. Mikao Usui was the principal of a Christian seminary in Kyoto, Japan, when he sought to duplicate the healing methods he thought were used by Jesus. He studied, meditated, prayed, and revived the ancient tradition. Some would call it blasphemy, and others would call it a miracle, but many Reiki receivers say that channeling "a divine energy flow" works to calm the mind and induce an altered state of relaxation.

Reiki therapists say anyone can learn to channel this energy, and you can even do it to yourself. In fact, many Reiki trainers require that you learn on yourself before you practice on others. If you were receiving a Reiki session, you would lie comfortably on a massage table while the therapist uses a series of hand positions just over or lightly touching your body. It takes about an hour to cover all the positions. They loosely correspond to where your chakras are located.

This energy work is said to rebalance the body mentally, physically, emotionally, and spiritually. It is used as a relaxation therapy, to stimulate the immune system, and to relieve pain.

Polarity

Freeing the energy flow via the chakras through subtle touching and gentle holding in a specific program that also includes exercise and nutrition is called polarity therapy. A combination of ancient and modern healing approaches, polarity was developed by Randolph Stone, who was born in 1890 in Austria. He moved to Chicago to study chiropractic, osteopathic, and naturopathic medicine, and spent years in India learning meditation and life energy.

5

Diversion

ARE WE HAVING FUN YET?

A study of older people by researchers at the Harvard University School of Public Health, published in the August 1999 issue of the *British Medical Journal*, concluded that there are health benefits in diversion. Physical activity has always been recommended as a way to stay healthy, but this study indicated that socializing may be as important for quality of life and extended life span.

People who like to eat out, play cards, go to the movies, attend religious services, and find new hobbies, to name but a few activities, live an average of two and a half years longer than more reclusive people, the study says. "That social activities involving almost no physical exertion played a measurable role at all in length of life is really quite something," says Thomas Glass, Harvard assistant professor of health and social behavior, who headed the study. "This is perhaps the strongest circumstantial evidence we've had to date that having a meaningful purpose at the end of life lengthens life. It may not be an old wives' tale after all."

Another study in the *British Medical Journal* followed more than fifteen thousand people for nine years to assess the association between longevity and attendance at cultural events. Even after adjusting for such factors as socioeconomic status, diet, exercise, disease, and smoking, researchers found a positive association.

At Carnegie Mellon University, a study found that a variety of social relationships helped people fend off colds. "Those with social ties demonstrated 20 percent greater immune function than those who didn't," says Bruce S. Rabin, coauthor of the study and director of the Brain, Behavior, and Immunity Center at the University of Pittsburgh. If you want to live longer and better, go out and do something fun with friends today.

146
✍

VACATIONS

Time and money are precious commodities, but fun is precious, too. Is fun time one of your priorities? Think of fun as therapy, and plan time out from your daily grind.

Spectrum magazine reported on a study performed by researchers at Tel Aviv University. They looked at billing and accounting employees to gauge whether vacations really offset work burnout. A two-week vacation led to a sharp decrease in exhaustion, but the benefits started to fall away after only three days back on the job. By three weeks, stress levels were back to normal. Since other studies indicate that vacations increase performance and minimize absenteeism, it is no wonder that travel professionals have acknowledged an increase in shorter, more frequent vacations than the formerly popular once-a-year, longer getaways. Whether you have the desire or resources to get away for only a day, or you dream and plan and save for a once-in-a-lifetime travel adventure, a change of pace and a different location may be just what the doctor ordered.

"While a vacation is certainly not a panacea for all that ails you," write Robert Ornstein, Ph.D., and David Sobel, M.D., in their book, *Healthy Pleasures*, "most people report relief from mental and physical stress. In one study, findings showed that getting away reduced fatigue, digestive problems, insomnia, and loss of interest in sex by half. Headaches plunged to 3 percent, compared to 21 percent before the vacation."

147

A vacation can be restful. For some, it means grabbing a deck chair or a beach towel and a good book and parking themselves for the duration. Others want excitement and adventure. Ecotours are stimulating and educational, a mind tonic. Some people choose mountain climbing or river rafting. Spa-goers might be looking for a wellness makeover. The proliferation of day spas makes it easy to enjoy a lunchtime or after-work mini-vacation. For the stress-relieving benefits of a vacation, a change of pace is the idea.

Retreats

Sometimes the purpose of a vacation is to find a quiet place to take stock of where you've been and where you want to go. A retreat "is a refreshing experience of withdrawing to a quiet place, alone or sometimes with a friend, to take a fresh look at life, to sort things out. How is life going? Where is it going? Where is God in all this?" says Retreats International, a network devoted to education, communication, and research in this area.

Retreats have traditionally been considered times of spiritual learning. Parables from all religions tell of people going off to the mountains or desert by themselves to gain wisdom and insight. Reflection and introspection are easier when we are secluded, away from the distractions of daily life.

Some retreat centers have policies of silence during various parts of the day. Others have spiritual or religious advisors available for personal counseling. There are retreats for couples who want to mend or enhance their relationships; retreats centered around themes for special-interest groups, like singles, youth groups, and clubs; and sanctuaries where individuals can go for self-examination and quiet time.

Although many retreat centers are maintained by members of a specific religious order, seekers from all faiths are usually welcome. Accommodations and dining are usually not fancy, but this is reflected in the attractive prices. The natural surroundings are meant to be comfortable but not too distracting. Retreats International says most large metropolitan areas have a retreat center within driving distance.

Retreat "resorts" offer natural settings with room to roam alone and still spend time with others exploring new experiences. In Hawaii, Terry Walker offers Dolphin Heart Women's Weeks, a time of "inner and outer adventures. Because the dolphins come when they choose and not when I schedule them, and the water is sometimes rough in the bay where they swim,

I cannot guarantee what will happen, but I do a dolphin presentation, snorkeling practice, and schedule lots of beach time," she says. "The retreat week is all about finding the power within, a refuge and a starting place from which to live your life the way you choose." Yoga, meditation, breathing practices, Watsu, and massage are part of the schedule.

At Kalani Oceanside Retreat, where Dolphin Weeks are held, they schedule by theme: For instance, hula, Pacific arts, men's and women's weeks, and gay men's and women's weeks are offered. At the Omega Institute for Holistic Studies in Rhinebeck, New York, you can learn spiritual drumming, yoga, ritual theater, communicating with animals, emotional intelligence, and many other esoteric studies with noted authors and experts. There are a number of yoga sanctuaries, art centers, and other retreat properties throughout the country.

149

SPAS

Destination Spas

Spas have long shed their reputations as fat farms and places to "dry out." They have become lifestyle universities, where people can learn how to live in a holistic, life-enhancing way. To that end, these places—where you can spend an extended time rejuvenating and revitalizing—feature not only stress-management and relaxation practices but also strategies for healthy nutrition, varied exercise programs, and extracurricular pursuits. Illness management, sports, outdoor challenge courses, art, music, dance, gardening, antiquing—anything to heal and stimulate mind, body, and spirit—are popular extracurricular activities at spas.

Most spas offer programs that integrate many of the topics in this book: relaxation, meditation, and breathing techniques; Ayurveda and aromatherapy; yoga, tai chi, and qigong; massage and hydrotherapy; nutrition and exercise.

Day Spas

You don't have to travel far to derive a spa's healthy benefits. Body treatments traditionally considered beauty and pampering services have proven to be relaxation enhancing and stress reducing. But massage and hydrotherapy, long known to be therapeutic, are not all that day spas offer. Spas today are becoming wellness clinics: Stress management, nutrition, and other wellness seminars are often available in addition to massage and beauty services. Breathing and meditation seminars are commonly offered. Many medical clinics and doctors' offices are now providing spa treatments as complementary adjuncts to allopathic therapies.

Reflexology massage is often given as an adjunct to pedicures and manicures for a relaxation-enhancing treatment. While you're being exfoliated and moisturized during a salt glow or loofah scrub, your muscles relax and your mind quiets—two important conditions of mindful relaxation. Being removed from noise and responsibility for the hour or so it takes to have a spa treatment can be as effective a relaxation tool as meditation. The growth in the number of day spas makes it relatively easy to find a place close to your home or office. Here are just a few more spa treatments that provide excellent relaxation experiences.

Abhayanga

Part of the Ayurvedic panchakarma purification therapy, this warm herbal oil massage is sometimes self-applied; at spas, this treatment is performed by two therapists simultaneously and is often followed by a hot-towel application.

Body Wrap

Linen sheets are steeped in an herbal tea, then wrapped around the body like a cocoon (leave your arms out if you're claustrophobic). Dry blankets or plastic sheeting is placed over the herbal sheets, and cool compresses are applied to the forehead while you rest for approximately half an hour. This practice is performed in a dimly lit room with New Age music or nature tapes playing softly.

Shirodhara

Shirodhara is an Ayurvedic treatment in which warm oil, custom-mixed with herbs and plants for each client's needs, is drizzled in a continuous flow onto the forehead—the "third eye" according to tradition—to calm and balance the nervous system.

Of course, an essential part of making time for a day spa or spa vacation is the affirmation that you are worth taking care of. Giving yourself an hour or a week for pampering is rejuvenating and healing.

151

HOME SANCTUARY

Even if you have acknowledged that you would benefit from meditation, time for introspection, or a long mineral bath, you may not have the ability or the wherewithal to really extricate yourself from your daily grind. Some people have created home sanctuaries, so that even if they have only five minutes at a time or five dollars in their pocket, a sacred space gives them instant access to a special getaway.

In many cultures, a home shrine is common. Typically religious in nature, they are intended to honor one's faith and ancestors. There is a trend, however, toward creating another kind of shrine, one to honor and acknowledge the value of self and serenity.

152

Try creating a space in the garden with a bench and a view of greenery to which you can escape for meditation, journaling, yoga, or just being. Even in a small home or apartment, you can designate a corner for your shrine. Take a comfortable chair or floor pillow, an aromatherapy candle, and pictures or objects that are significant to you, and create an alcove that you have consciously set aside as a place for you to be with you, to meditate. Give yourself a massage. If you don't have to share it, a bathroom with a tub is a good location. There are many products available from retail, catalog, and on-line sources to assemble all you need to make your own spa day at home.

Whether you explore your thoughts in your sanctuary or allow them to dissipate while you relax, this unique place helps signal your mind and body that this is a special time just for you. It's a way of giving yourself permission and encouragement to take the time and space you need to counter your stressors.

PETS

Dog owners know how it feels to come home to the eager, welcoming face of unconditional love. Cat owners usually have to work a little harder for an expression of gratitude from their pets. For some people, it's a tropical aquarium or a cuddly bunny rabbit, a horse, or a tortoise. Whatever animal is the object of your affection, if you have one you know the joys of owning a pet.

Several studies have indicated that people who own pets live longer and happier lives. Petting and stroking an animal lowers blood pressure and heart attack risk. Heart attack patients who have a dog to walk when they return home from the hospital have seven times the survival rate of like patients who don't have pets.

A study in the *Journal of Personality and Social Psychology* reported that pet ownership by elderly people can reduce psychological distress. Judith M. Siegel, Ph.D., of the University of California, Los Angeles (UCLA), conducted the study of Medicare patients, more than a third of whom owned dogs, cats, birds, or fish. After controlling the data for other factors, Siegel found that pet owners made fewer visits to doctors' offices. "Pets seem to help their owners in times of stress by providing companionship and comfort they might otherwise seek from physicians," she says.

UCLA and other hospitals and clinics have programs in which animals visit patients. Pet-assisted therapy allows patients to forget their pain and push themselves a little harder and longer when exercising. Dogs are most often used with physical therapy and rehabilitation patients, and at UCLA they cheer up people who've been waiting months for organ transplants. Stroke patients with limited arm movement have shown improvement after brushing or playing tug-of-war with a dog. The Delta Society in Portland, Oregon, says it has more than twenty-five hundred pet partner teams in forty-five states.

According to the Delta Society, a group that acts as a clearinghouse for pet therapy programs, part of the reason animal companionship works is that it is culturally acceptable to give affection to an animal and an easy way to facilitate conversation with others. Pets are nonjudgmental companions, and having to care for their daily needs gives meaning and purpose to one's life. An NIH study noted that pet therapy benefits among patients included increased smiling, increased conversations, physical and emotional reaching out to the animal, improved alertness and attention, a greater sense of well-being, and lessened depression.

154

EXPRESSIVE ARTS THERAPIES

"When you're in a 'stuck place' or trying to make a decision, expressive arts therapies can be a good tool to help draw out your thoughts and emotions," says therapist Barbara Shaw. Shaw says dance movement, art, music, journaling, and other expressions can access the limbic systems, where the emotions are. "Their effectiveness is in switching your channels from the rational mind to the unconscious."

Art Therapy

Shaw says you can use pencil, paint, clay, or any art medium to help you discover underlying feelings that you may be having trouble identifying. "Just draw, don't think about it," she says.

You can also sculpt, model, paste, paint. Switching from right to left brain, or the other way, will put you on a path of discovery and give you a new perspective.

Art therapy doesn't have to be a formal thing, although there are therapists who specialize in it. Many people start to doodle when their minds need a breather. Schools, community centers, and neighborhood parks are good places to find classes if you would want instruction in a particular medium.

Music Therapy

William Congreve wrote, "Music has charms to soothe a savage breast." Therapists agree. Music therapy is used by medical experts to help patients relax before and after surgery, during psychoanalysis, during testing procedures, and for relaxation and healing. Research in the operating room shows that music stimulates the production of endorphins.

"Music is not only indigenous to culture, it is indigenous to the human soul," says Linda M. Hynds, R.N., P.N.P., whose company, Gaining Perspective, teaches stress-management workshops. "Every culture since the beginning of time has had some type of music. Today we have noise pollution from traffic, industry, the constant buzz of various media, electromagnetic fields, and human voices shouting and arguing, which affect us all on a daily basis. Music can aid us in finding equilibrium and balance."

Music therapy is an enhancement to relaxation and meditation skills, says Hynds. If you practice relaxation daily, it can annul or mitigate the effects of accumulated stress responses. In a synthesis of many studies, Shirley Thompson, Ph.D., at the University of South Carolina's School of Public Health concluded

155

that noise can trigger the body's stress response, resulting in an increase in blood pressure. "Music can evoke emotional and sensual responses, comfort and calm, or stimulate creativity and excitement," Hynds says. "It can aid in releasing emotion from past experiences."

Hynds quotes George Gershwin: "Music sets up a certain vibration which unquestionably results in a physical reaction. Eventually, the proper vibration for every person will be found and utilized."

The American Music Therapy Association says everyone can benefit from music therapy: children, adolescents, adults, and the elderly; people with mental-health issues; or those who have physical, developmental, and learning disabilities, Alzheimer's, substance abuse problems, or chronic pain.

Intensive-care patients on ventilators who had music therapy showed significantly less anxiety and slower heart and respiration rates (indicating greater relaxation) than those who did not have access to the thirty minutes of music. In the journal *Heart Lung*, a study concluded that "even a single music therapy session was found to be effective for decreasing anxiety and promoting wellness."

Musician and music producer Steven Halpern, Ph.D., began studying music "not only as an art form but as a vehicle for self-transcendence." He wanted to become so proficient on his instruments that his higher self could come through. During many years as a professional musician, he kept looking for a kind of music "that would help people reconnect with their own nature. Suddenly, I began hearing music in my head—not the usual jazz and blues, but a floating, ethereal music with no rhythm," he says. "It was not a music derived from my intellectual studies, but as if I had tapped into a wavelength that was broadcasting the Music of the Spheres . . . as if I weren't personally creating it but receiving it."

When Halpern began playing this new music, people reported feeling meditative and relaxed after hearing it, and so he began studying psychoacoustics, the physics and psychology of sound. He has continued his studies, and says that most people learn better when they are relaxed, and certain kinds of music truly can enhance healing, concentration, retention, and performance over an extended period of time. Halpern produces and records a line of therapeutic music such as *Sound Health: The Music and Sounds That Make Us Whole* for his company, Inner Peace Music.

157

Tom Kenyon, M.A., author of *Brain States,* is the founder of Acoustic Brain Research, which documents the effects of sound and music on the human nervous system. Paul Overman, Ph.D., is the director of QuantumLink, a consortium of health professionals and researchers focusing on mind–body psychoacoustics. They produced *The Ultimate Brain*, a four-CD series in which pulses of sound are embedded into a musical soundtrack "enticing the listener's brain waves to lock on to specific frequencies" to lead the mind into states of consciousness appropriate to relaxation, creativity, health, and performance.

You all know the power of music. It evokes memories, can make you sad or happy, pensive or perturbed. "Music moves in intangible ways," says music therapist Miriam Witkin of Light Productions. "When you add lyrics, music becomes a powerful tool for sending messages to the brain. Possibly, new truths are heard and felt. If the music and lyrics are meaningful, "new wisdom is reaching our minds, planting seeds. Our thinking can alter. Music can impart positive, affirming, healthy messages."

Dance Therapy

Dancing as therapy is as old as tribal ritual. A formal approach to dance therapy began in the United States in the early 1940s, and by 1956 there were enough dance therapists to form the American Dance Therapy Association. The group publishes a journal that develops guidelines and monitors its standards.

158

Dance therapy allows people to express their emotions through movement to music. It has been shown to be clinically effective for decreasing tension, anxiety, fear, and depression; reducing chronic pain; enhancing respiratory and circulatory functions; promoting healing; increasing self-esteem; improving body image; and enhancing communication skills.

Mindful Movement

"Emotions are like weather. Once they are expressed they change and move on," says dance therapist Françoise Netter. "If we take apart the word *emotion* we have 'e-motion,' energy in motion. To keep the energy moving in our emotions, we need to have appropriate outlets of expression. Many people work out to release pent-up emotions, but feelings can also be expressed more directly and beneficially in Mindful Movement; specific feelings are identified and then given the opportunity to be fully expressed."

Netter says that "in Mindful Movement, we manipulate time, space, energy, motion, and rhythm [the principles of dance] to better understand the stages of our lives. Stress, in energetic terms, is a backlog. We've overloaded our systems and feel off balance, scattered, disconnected. We may be moving so fast that, like a car out of control, we're desperately steering to keep from crashing. All these experiences can be expressed physically. In moving mindfully, we can allow these moods, feelings, and energy flows the freedom to express, explore, and change shape, space, and dimension. We not only release stagnant thoughts and feelings, we also allow them to evolve in an organic and self-contained manner."

159

ℒ❤

JOURNALING

Human beings need to communicate. Several investigations have shown that revealing a secret trauma can relieve stress and improve health. But not everyone finds it easy or desirable to confide feelings to others. Writing in a journal regularly can provide an outlet to enable you to "power cope," as James W. Pennebaker, M.D., writes in his book, *Opening Up: The Healing Power of Confiding in Others*. Journaling works well in conjunction with other techniques, such as meditation. First you reduce stress symptoms by relaxation, then you can use the writing to help resolve the problems that make you tense.

"Writing about thoughts and feelings associated with a traumatic experience can help you get past it," says Pennebaker. "Writing can also act as preventive maintenance. The value of writing our thoughts and feelings lies in reducing inhibition and organizing our complicated mental and emotional lives."

> **Journaling**
>
> If you think keeping a journal would be a good stress-management technique for you and don't know how to start, Dr. Pennebaker suggests, "Focus on issues you are living with—experiences you find yourself thinking or dreaming about too much of the time. Find a place where you can be undisturbed. Let go, and write about your deepest emotions for fifteen or twenty minutes at a time. The only rule is to write continuously during that time. You don't have to worry about grammar—write just for yourself, as though you were going to throw this away."
>
> Source: James W. Pennebaker, M.D., *Opening Up: The Power of Confiding in Others.* Used with permission.

"Many of us are so busy that we take our cell phones to the beach on our 'vacations,' and get panicked if we haven't checked our E-mail in twenty-four hours," says Eldonna Bouton, author of *Write Away: A Journal Writing Tool Kit* and *Loose Ends: A Journaling Tool for Tying Up the Incomplete Details of Your Life and Heart.* "When was the last time you took inventory of your thoughts and emotions, or spent twenty minutes alone with your thoughts?" she asks.

"Journaling is an excellent way to not only reconnect with your 'lost self,' but it also forces you to slow down, reflect, and allow yourself a means to unravel the tangle of emotion-packed experiences within each day," Bouton says. She thinks of her journal as her "pocket therapist. At least once a day, I dump the 'Cosmic Trash' that continually rolls around in my head," she says. "By facing my fears on the page, they lose their power over me, and I find myself calmer, more relaxed. I let the stress flow out of the pen and lighten the burden of the unspoken."

It's not always pretty writing. "Often, my words are just a mess of whining and sniveling," Bouton says. "Once in a while, a poetic gem will spill onto the page. Having the opportunity to tap into the creative well within is just an added bonus."

161

Deepak Chopra writes for an hour a day. It's a way of dealing with thoughts and feelings. Sometimes it turns into materials for his books, but always it serves as an outlet, a way of clarifying thoughts and feelings.

When Linda Ann Olson became a mother for the first time, journaling helped her cope with the stress. "I found that writing down my prayers, hopes, fears, challenges, and dreams gave me an outlet for my feelings and emotions, which helped to reduce the stress of caring for twins," she says. "A journal is a private place where you are free to express yourself as you choose." For Olson, God is an important part of that expression. "Through prayer, you know you can handle anything that comes along." For her, a journal is a form of conversational prayer that helps her stay committed to what she says is the toughest and most important job on Earth: being a good mother. Olson collected her thoughts, prayers, and ideas, and created a book, *New Psalms for New Moms: A Keepsake Journal.*

In April 1999, a study in the *Journal of the American Medical Association* reported that cathartic writing helped patients suffering from asthma and rheumatoid arthritis reduce debilitating physical symptoms. The participants who wrote about traumatic events in their lives showed a boost in T cell production (immunity protection), lower blood pressure, easing of symptoms, fewer sick days, and fewer doctor visits. "These gains were beyond those attributable to the standard medical care that all participants were receiving," says Joshua M. Smyth, Ph.D., of North Dakota State University in Fargo. He and the study's other authors say a growing amount of literature suggests that addressing patients' psychological needs produces both psychological and physical health benefits. Expressive writing is one such technique that has been used successfully in several controlled studies.

Louise DeSalvo, professor of English and creative writing at Hunter College, says, "I regularly witness the physical and emotional transformation of my students. I see how they change physically and psychically when they work on writing projects—diary, memoir, fiction, poetry, biographical essays—that grow from a deep, authentic place, when they confront the pain in their work." Her book, *Writing as a Way of Healing: How Telling Our Stories Transforms Our Lives*, discusses how famous authors from Ray Bradbury to Virginia Woolf have used writing to deal creatively with their stressors.

Top Ten Miraculous Benefits of Keeping a Journal

1. *Clarify your goals:* As you write a few thoughts each day, your ideas about what is important, what is worthy of your life and your time will become much clearer. You'll automatically discover what you really want in life.

2. *Simplify your life:* Spending as little as ten minutes with pen and paper describing your values, noting your achievements, and giving thanks for the joys of life will make you less tolerant of life's distractions. Things become simpler when you write them down.

3. *Strengthen your relationships:* Keeping a journal will give you time and the words to express your feelings, help you understand and be patient with your loved ones' peccadilloes, and teach you to love more powerfully.

4. *Make yourself more attractive:* Socrates said, "Know thyself." Keeping a journal will help you know yourself and express yourself more clearly, and that is amazingly attractive!

5. *Empower yourself:* Thinking with pen and paper forces you to eliminate fuzzy or confusing images and to "laser in"

163

continued on next page

on precisely the right word, the most powerful image to express yourself. Keeping a journal will make you a better communicator, and that can make you rich.

6. *Eliminate temptation:* Some ideas sound great in our imagination, but when written on paper they just aren't the same. It's easy to blurt out, "I hate my job," but writing about what it means to quit, change careers, and start over will quickly result in one of two things: The temptation will go away, or you'll start generating actual plans to make your life better. Either way, you win!

7. *Reaffirm the reality of your life:* Writing about life adds meaning and power. Journaling about your child's first steps or first tooth, first day of school, first date, and high school graduation adds substance to these milestones. A friend of mine just became a grandfather for the first time, and gave his son, the proud father, a fat three-ring binder of notes he'd written as he'd watched his baby boy grow for twenty-five years. Together they cried and laughed at the reality that life is a sacred, wonderful thing.

8. *Help yourself be quiet:* Journaling has been called a form of meditation. It has a similar power to quiet the mind and

focus your thoughts. It even has the power to turn off the TV. It can heal anxiety, change your breathing, and make you smile. What more could you ask?

9. *Help yourself speak out:* Many of my articles, letters to the local paper, and letters to friends began as notes in my journal. A journal helps ideas become words, and it provides a nursery for words to grow into sentences and paragraphs, until finally they need a stage on which to express themselves. Sometimes that stage is a candlelit dinner, other times it's a protest sign or a letter to an old friend. Whatever form it takes, many of those messages would never have been born without the safety of a journal in which to grow.

10. *Finally, a journal just feels good:* Using quality paper and a fountain pen or other beautiful instrument with just the right heft and feel is a wonderfully sensuous, delightful experience. It will cheer you up, reduce your stress, make you smile, and add to your life. Who knows, it may even improve your sex life or make you more patient with the kids! (Well, it might!)

165

Adapted from Philip E. Humbert, Ph.D., www.philiphumbert.com/Articles/10Journal.html. Used with permission.

ENTERTAINMENT THERAPY

All media can provide an escape from your own reality, yet sometimes it isn't escape you need but support or validation. "When you see a movie whose character is going through a life scenario like yours, it may help you to understand you are not the only one who's ever lived through something like this," says actor Zelda Rubenstein, best known for her roles in the movies *Poltergeist* and *16 Candles* and on television's *Picket Fences.* "People go to the movies and watch television because it helps take them out of their own lives for a little while.

"When they are locked into an uncomfortable situation, it can help to see how other people or characters react to or resolve their problems." Rubenstein has conquered her own challenges as a "little person," refusing to let being different keep her from living a full and creative life. "We can get inspiration from seeing how others face their dilemmas and fight their monsters," she says.

If you read a book whose characters are traveling to places you'll never visit but long to know about, you can feel as if you've been away and learned a lot. Maybe you'd like to throw a pie in your boss's face, yell at your mother-in-law, let the air out of someone's tires, kiss a stranger, or run away to a desert island. Fiction can give you a sense of vicarious revenge, pleasure, life. Documentaries can inspire knowledge, gratitude, caring, and action.

Song lyrics, poetry, movie scripts, and television plots can actually help you zone out or tune in to yourself, depending on what you need in a given moment. A concert is a kind of group therapy—the audience is joined for the evening by a shared sense of appreciation for an artist or group. When the lights go down in the theater and the orchestra starts to play, the sense of expectation and excitement of traveling to another world does it for me. "The theater experience is not too different in some ways than that in a church or synagogue," says Gordon Davidson, artistic director/producer of the Center Theatre Group/Mark Taper Forum/Ahmanson Theatre in Los Angeles, California. "People come together to share something in common, to celebrate the rituals of life.

"Some complain that theater should be used [only] for entertainment," Davidson says, "but I see entertainment as a more embracing word, one that includes joy and pain. . . . A larger pattern or interconnected theme seems to emerge from individual plays: the universal desire to achieve and protect a relationship, and the central importance of the family in the life of the individual . . . recognizable human beings trying to deal with their frailties, to survive undamaged, to treat each other with as much love and respect as possible in the sometimes lonely individual pursuit of happiness."

Despite Davidson's heavy schedule, he makes time for theater because it enhances his life. "I believe in theater, I enjoy it, it nurtures me," he says. "Some jobs suck out your energy, your happiness. For me, theater is a great source of energy, joy, learning ways of confronting questions about oneself, the world, relationships."

167

HOBBIES

Engaging in a pastime is a time-honored part of a balanced lifestyle. Its very definition is "something that amuses and serves to make time pass agreeably." Hobbies work simply by taking your mind off the stresses of the day, giving you something fun to do, and diverting your thoughts away from the negative and toward the positive.

Some people would say playing golf creates as much stress as diversion, but generally pastimes are a source of accomplishment and enjoyment, a pursuit important to holistic health. A study commissioned by the Home Sewing Association showed that sewing, for example, lowered heart rate and led to an improved sense of well-being.

If you haven't picked up those knitting needles, planted new flowers, read a new book, built a bookcase, or gone for a boat ride in quite some time, plan some recreational activity for next weekend. Pursuing one's hobbies is an easy way to manage stress. Spending an hour at something you like may lessen your feelings of tiredness and tension.

SOCIAL SUPPORT

A 1999 study published in the journal *Psychosomatic Medicine* said that social isolation, lack of social support, and a tendency to suppress anger were associated with decreased heart rate variability (HRV)—a marker of how the body handles stress. Previous studies have linked decreased HRV to vulnerability to diseases such

168

as atherosclerosis and coronary heart disease, and to higher mortality rates. The authors said the results of this study of healthy Swedish women suggest HRV may be a mediating factor in the relationship of social isolation and suppressed anger to health.

Another psychoneuroimmunology study from Drs. Janice Kiecolt-Glaser and Ronald Glaser compared students' immune systems before exams. Those students who considered themselves to be lonely had more suppression of the natural T cell activity that protects the immune system. The inference is that other emotional conditions can damage our ability to protect our immune systems, for example, if we are suffering from stress as a result of HIV, chronic pain or illness, the death of a loved one, or divorce.

In the 1970s, a notable study at Stanford University involved support groups for women with advanced stages of breast cancer. Led by Irvin D. Yalom, M.D., using his technique called "supportive-expressive group therapy," and with David Spiegel, a Stanford psychiatrist, the study demonstrated that those women who saw themselves as receiving or having support had more positive immune system responses and lived twice as long as those who felt they had no support. It was a simple presentation: The women simply expressed their emotions about cancer in the context of group support.

Support doesn't have to come from a group. One good friend or family member in whom you can confide and share experiences may be enough. When you are under stress and lose sight of the big picture, a friend can help you put things in perspective. Sometimes just saying things out loud helps you to refocus and prioritize. A caring friend will help you shed

169

counterproductive guilt. A buddy who really understands can help ease the tension just because you know you're not alone. Friends can help you give yourself permission to take the time to nurture yourself; often when you need it most is when you think you have the least time.

When your friends trust you to listen when they are having trouble coping, there is comfort in knowing that others have weathered the bad times. If problems just seem to be too big for you and your friends to get under control, organized support groups provide practical advice for dealing with specific situations: grief, illness, divorce, substance abuse, gambling, eating disorders, physical and emotional disabilities—the list is as long as the human condition is complicated.

170

Chances are, if you're socially isolated it's because the pain of loneliness is more comfortable than taking the risk in sharing your story, possibly inviting criticism or rejection. Know that you are not alone in your suffering, and there are people out there more like you than you might think.

It's cliché but true: To have a friend you have to be a friend. Commit to a support group, class, club, or volunteer organization, and you're sure to make new friends who have things in common. Community centers, local hospitals, wellness clinics, and universities host many kinds of support groups. Most states have programs, and you can contact the National Self-Help Clearinghouse for referral.

6

Changing Perspective

The way you think influences your physiological state. And the way you express yourself can affect the way you feel, sometimes to your detriment. Perspective is everything. When you communicate, you may be speaking from internalized experiences that you assume the other person will relate to and understand. Miscommunication and frustration can result, and stress naturally follows.

Meditation, breathing, and other relaxation techniques can help you gain perspective and develop insight. They work because when you quiet your mind and relax your body, you can see things more clearly. "Most of our minds are so clouded or disturbed with disruptive thinking, we would not recognize peace of mind were it to occur," says Lloyd J. Thomas, Ph.D., psychologist and personal coach. "Have you ever rediscovered a clear lake in the early morning?" he asks. "The surface is so still, it perfectly reflects the trees, clouds, and sky around it. You can see the rocks resting on the bottom. The lake is in its natural pristine state, unclouded and accurately reflecting the image of the world. Later in the day, if you were to return to that same lake, it might not be so serene and reflective. Wind, boats, and swimmers are disturbing the surface and distorting what is reflected. Silt floats in the water, clouding it and making it impossible to see the bottom.

"Our minds are very much like the lake," Thomas says. "When they are still, they are more accurately reflective of reality. When they are not clouded, we are able to 'see' the depths of our own awareness. But most of the time, our minds are disturbed with activities of daily living which disrupt the clarity of our awareness of reality. They are filled with emotional disruption which clouds our perceptions."

172

LEARNED OPTIMISM

Some people just seem to get up on the right side of the bed, and others don't. There may be psychophysiological reasons, but they are not insurmountable. If you try to look on the bright side, things really may get better. The American Psychological Association says, "People who learn to maintain an optimistic attitude may not only avoid depression, they may actually improve their physical health."

A study of freshmen at the University of Pennsylvania, conducted by Martin Seligman, Ph.D., and Gregory Buchanan, Ph.D., invited students identified by a questionnaire as "most pessimistic" to take part. They were randomly assigned to either a sixteen-hour workshop or a control group. The workshop participants learned to dispute their chronic negative thoughts and were taught social and work skills to help avert depression. After an eighteen-month follow-up, the workshop students reported fewer physical problems and were more active in maintaining their health.

Happiness and the Immune System

"Previous scientific experiments have observed a correlation between changing moods and the immune system," says David Warburton, professor and head of the department of psycho-pharmacology at Reading University in England. Warburton is also founder of the Association for Research into the Science of Enjoyment (ARISE). ARISE undertook a study, which showed that within twenty minutes of having happy thoughts, the amount of antibody immunoglobulins in a group of people doubled, and stayed higher for at least three hours. Conversely, those who focused on traumatic or painful memories had lowered levels. "These new studies provide a direct causal link, and identifying this direct link proves that happiness can make you healthier," Warburton says.

173

RITUAL

Rituals are religious or social practices that provide security in the face of chaos. Habitually reading the morning paper can be a ritual. If, on a given day, you cannot do so, you may feel out of

A Native American Way of Coping

For close to two decades, Joyce C. Mills, Ph.D., author of *Reconnecting to the Magic of Life,* has learned many healing approaches from Native American people. With their permission, she has respectfully integrated many of these philosophies along with her own to healing. One she recommends for coping with grief can be adapted to let go of any negative emotions.

Mills tells the story of Maria who was diagnosed with breast cancer and then underwent successful surgery and immediate breast reconstruction. She handled the situation well, until she was told that another mammogram indicated a possible problem, and she had to have another surgery. Again she went back to life as usual, until one day she began to cry uncontrollably. She remained agitated and couldn't sleep.

Maria found her way to The Turtle Island Project, a healing retreat that Mills cofacilitates with Mona Polacca, M.S.W., and Charles Etta Sutton, M.S.W. With the insight afforded by that experience, Maria recognized she'd never allowed herself to experience the grief, never said good-bye to what was such a special part of her body; she realized she was in mourning. Mills observes

174

that some people think just moving on past a loss makes it go away, but the unconscious mind knows better. Maria may have thought her implants would fool her body into thinking nothing was missing, but she needed emotional healing, too.

The Native American leaders suggested a ritual for closure, for healing, for saying good-bye. You can adapt this ritual to say good-bye to anything or anyone you have lost. Give yourself some quiet time alone, and write a letter to that someone or something, as Maria did to her breasts. Create a sacred space: Clear a table, and arrange it with objects meaningful to you—a rock, a gem, a flower—and keep writing until you feel you've expressed everything there is to say.

Take your letter to a favorite outdoor place. Sit on the ground, and as the sun sets, read the letter aloud. Give yourself time to connect to the earth and sky. Then make a small hole in the ground, and bury the letter. Imagine the breeze carrying your words up to the Creator of the Universe, or however you feel comfortable imagining letting go.

Breathe deeply and slowly, and listen to the sounds around you. Mother Nature's message will come to you. You will begin to heal.

sorts. Family dinners are ritual gatherings, as are going to church or temple and the annual Fourth of July picnic. We have expectations that we will enjoy these rituals in a particular way, and there is comfort in that.

A ritual can be healing, as they traditionally have been in many cultures, such as Native American. You can make your own ritual to "right the wrongs" of your past, speak your silent heart, start to control the way you react to things, redub the old tapes— cognitive reframing.

Native American Sweat Lodge

176

The Native American Sweat Lodge can take place in a lodge made of canvas over a wood frame, in a cave, or even in a sauna. Lava rocks are heated with water to very high temperatures. People may beat drums or chant. Participants sit in a circle and tell their stories. The stories chosen are often meant to let others know where you are coming from, and the dark, hot, intimate atmosphere often brings up stories you didn't even know you had to tell.

"The lava rocks that bring in the heat are actually our grandfathers, and their breath is the steam that is created when the rocks are splashed with water. The steam helps you see through your fear and makes you strong," says Howard D. Silverman, M.D., coauthor (with Carl Hammerschlag, M.D.) of *Healing Ceremonies: Creating Personal Rituals for Spiritual, Emotional, Physical and Mental Health.* This was explained to him by Hopi medicine man Bill Tyner, known as Sigee (uncle).

After his first experience with this ritual, which he discovered while searching for a way to touch the hearts as well as the bodies of his patients, Silverman said, "The ceremony was beautiful. I was moved by the prayers which these 'relatives' offered for me and my family, for my health and strength, for wisdom. . . . That sweat lodge ceremony had helped drain me of some of my fear and rigidity, the instructions and attitudes I'd been accumulating like a side effect of my medical training: Don't introduce yourself by your first name, and maintain an objective, detached, impersonal relationship. That ceremony fanned the spark that had very nearly been extinguished—my connection to the power to heal with joy."

HUMOR

Laughter is contagious—and healing. It reduces stress, releases tension, and can help you loosen up, see things from another side, and gain perspective. Science has caught up with proof of its positive side effects. Laughter relaxes muscles; stimulates the respiratory system; boosts endorphin production; decreases cortisol levels; increases heart, blood pressure, and circulatory rates; decreases the intensity of pain and unhappiness; and can speed healing.

Norman Cousins, former editor of the *Saturday Review*, started the serious investigation of laughter's effects when he turned to humor to help him get through the sudden onset of a debilitating illness. In his 1979 book, *Anatomy of an Illness,* Cousins documented his unhappiness with how traditional medicine wasn't helping his condition, and told how he discovered laughter as a way to regain his ability to move freely without chronic pain. The book was written in response to the many people who asked him "whether it was true that I laughed my way out of a crippling disease that doctors believed to be irreversible." He went on to live relatively well for another twenty-six years.

Margie Ingram, M.A., Ed. Spec., directs special programs at the HUMOR Project—"promoting the positive power of humor and creativity in everyday life and work"—and coordinates its annual International Humor Conference. Long involved with stress-management training, Ingram says, "We can use humor to tickle stress before it tackles us. In fact, physiological research over the past forty years tells us that when we laugh, a lot of good things happen inside: respiration and circulation are enhanced, stress-related hormones are suppressed, and the immune system is activated. Laughter is indeed the jest medicine."

Ingram is the partner and wife of Joel Goodman, founder of the American Humor Association (AHA!) and the HUMOR Project. In 1977, Goodman's father, Arthur Herndon, suffered an aortic aneurysm; the situation was so serious that he was flown to Houston to see the famous Dr. Michael DeBakey. While Goodman was on the way to the hospital on a shuttle, a magician named Alvin did his performance thing, and Goodman enjoyed it despite his angst. He thought, "Do we have to wait for the Alvins to make our lives brighter?" He formed the HUMOR Project "not to analyze humor to death, but rather to look for practical ways of bringing humor to life."

178

Positive Thinking: How to Use the Power of Thought to Control Pain

If you're in pain, you can immediately decrease your agony, reduce your need for medication, heal more quickly, and possibly even live longer.

The secret? Attitude adjustment.

The power of positive thinking isn't an optimist's fairy tale. At Johns Hopkins Hospital, scientists are now studying and harnessing the mind's tremendous power to control pain.

Elementary biology teaches that pain is a purely physiological reaction: Burn yourself or sprain an ankle, and nerve endings send chemical signals racing to your brain. The brain responds to these signals with a burst of sensation we call pain. While this scenario is basically correct, it leaves out one of the most important aspects of pain perception: emotions.

While pain itself is an affective state fed by biological mechanisms, it is magnified or diminished by emotion. In other words, pain results in unpleasant physical sensation, but your emotional state affects how you interpret or perceive that pain.

Goodman says, "I take my work seriously, and myself lightly. In helping people to get smileage out of their jobs and life, I agree with Victor Borge's notion that 'a smile is the shortest distance between two people.'"

Humor has been used as a self-defense mechanism for some personalities, and for them it may be a form of verbal outlet. Obviously, though, the highest benefits of laughter come when humor is used as a tool, rather than a weapon; that is, laughing *with* others, not *at* others. In an essay published in the *Journal of the American Medical Association*, Goodman wrote, "Humor is laughter made from pain, not pain inflicted by laughter."

"Humor can be a positive and powerful ally as we schlep through life. We can use comic vision to face stressful situations. Ask yourself how your favorite comedian would look at it; often, that makes it easy to reframe it into a laughing matter. We have to learn to laugh at ourselves," Goodman says. "Of course, some of us have more material to work with than others."

ANGER MANAGEMENT

Some people get angrier faster and more intensely than others. Others don't express their anger outwardly but instead suppress it and take it out on themselves. This can lead to high blood pressure, depression, and other physical problems. When suppressed anger is expressed in passive-aggressive ways, it can put rifts in relationships. Healthy people can convert anger into positive, constructive behaviors. Stress-management techniques and relaxation therapies can help you calm yourself down and avoid the negative results of expressing anger inappropriately.

Anger can range from irritation to rage, and feelings of anger result in the old fight-or-flight reactions: increased adrenaline, heart rate, and blood pressure. Here's what the April 1999 issue of the *Mayo Clinic Women's Health Source* newsletter says happens when you get angry:

- Your heart races, and your blood pressure soars.
- Arteries dilate to carry more blood to your muscles.
- Your platelets get stickier to help prevent you from bleeding to death if you're wounded.
- Over time, repeated angry episodes can attack your artery walls and eventually cause your arteries to clog with plaque.
- A surge of blood can cause a plaque to dislodge and block an artery farther downstream. The clotting material your body sends to repair the damage can block the artery even more, setting you up for a heart attack or a dangerous heart rhythm. This is especially true if you already have heart trouble. In fact, a Harvard study of 1,600 women and men found that the risk of another heart attack doubled during or after an episode of anger.

181

"Anger is a completely human, normal, and healthy human emotion," according to the APA. "But when it gets out of control and turns destructive, it can lead to problems: problems at work, in your personal relationships, and in the overall quality of your life. And it can make you feel as though you are at the mercy of an unpredictable and powerful emotion."

If you have a problem with anger management, you know it. You may have a genetic or physiological predisposition to

anger; if so, you've probably heard stories about your short temper from family members. We are often conditioned to think of
anger as a bad thing, and that can make some of us direct the
anger in inappropriate and self-defeating ways. Here's what the
Mayo Clinic newsletter said about "turning down the heat when
you feel yourself starting to boil":

- Be aware that you have a choice in how you respond
  to situations. With practice, you can choose not to
  get angry.
- Figure out what triggers your anger.
- Talk to yourself. What's really causing your anger and
  is it important? Tell yourself to calm down and not to
  yell or strike out.
- Express your frustration calmly. Words spoken in anger
  will cause stress reactions in your body. The same
  words spoken calmly won't.
- Walk away and take deep breaths. Come back when
  you're calm.
- Try to understand the other person's point of view,
  and listen without anger.
- Don't assume people are out to get you.

When we've been taught not to be angry, we don't learn
how to use anger constructively. Deep breathing, visualization,
guided imagery, journaling, lucid dreaming, yoga, and regular
exercise all can help us manage our anger in positive ways.
Cognitive reframing—changing your perspective, putting yourself in the other person's shoes—is a good way to defuse anger.
This is a big-sounding phrase for a simple idea: seeing the glass

half-full or half-empty. When you have a problem or stressful situation, looking at things from another perspective may give you insight into yourself and others. Cognitive reframing, for nonpsychiatry professionals, is very close to the concept of "restructuring," that is, being aware of the way you may react to a situation (to which you learn there is another side), striving to be aware of your learned behavior, acknowledging it, and restructuring your reaction to it.

Jeffrey Deffenbacher, Ph.D., who specializes in anger management, offers this tip for when you're feeling very angry: "Picture yourself as a god or goddess, a supreme ruler who owns the streets and stores and office space, striding along and having your way in all situations while others defer to you. The more detail you can get into your imaginary scenes, the more chances you'll have to realize that maybe you are being a little unreasonable; you'll also realize how unimportant the things you're angry about really are."

183

For a while, it was popular to vent your rage by hitting a pillow or fighting with padded bats. Now it is thought that encouraging such angry outbursts is more harmful than helpful. Redirecting your energy into positive behaviors such as exercise and stress-management techniques is far more constructive.

If your anger is frequently out of control, seek help from a qualified therapist. Group therapy is often beneficial. If you just have a few too many days when anger gets in the way of your life, your relaxation, and your well-being, give yourself a break. Take time-outs, make space between appointments, and take time to get where you're going. Practice relaxation techniques daily.

Expressing your anger assertively, not aggressively, is the healthiest way to get those feelings out. "To do this, you have to learn to make clear what your needs are, and how to get them met, without hurting others. Being assertive," says the APA, "doesn't mean being pushy or demanding; it means being respectful of yourself and others."

ASSERTIVENESS TRAINING

Many responsibilities are impossible to avoid, but we do have a choice about some. Saying yes to an invitation, a favor, or a chore when you really want to say no can be more than momentarily stressful; it can lead to suppressed anger and hostility. NIH studies point to these feelings as a risk factor in high blood pressure and heart disease. The consequences to your emotional health are well documented. Remember that to care for others you need to nurture yourself. Sometimes you just have to say no.

Learning to say no may be the first step in asserting yourself, but this coping skill goes far beyond a single word. Assertiveness training teaches you to confront situations head-on instead of being afraid, intimidated, frustrated, and stressed out. It's a technique designed to give you more control over what you say and do. Many colleges and community centers offer assertiveness training classes. You can check with local mental-health facilities as well.

Learn to Say No

The most important thing you can do for yourself in a crisis situation is to learn to manage your time. You have to put yourself first. Whether you're healthy or trying to heal, ask yourself: Is this what I want to put my time into right now? Whenever you find yourself in a life crisis, ask the following questions:

- Who are the most important people in my life?
- Am I investing my time in the people and things that matter most to me, both for healing and for living a meaningful life?
- If not, what am I willing to do about that?

You may need to cut down on the time you spend with people whose orientation and behavior no longer fit in with your need to heal. Using time wisely also means leaving empty space for yourself, time to do nothing so that you allow new ideas and feelings to come to the surface. An illness, a trauma, or a life crisis can become an opportunity to explore life at a slower pace.

185

Source: Caroline Myss, "Healing: Why We Don't...and How We Can," www.myss.com/feat__naj_heal6.html. Used with permission.

WOMEN AND STRESS

Science has proven that premenstrual syndrome, painful menstruation, perimenopause, and menopause are sometimes accompanied by symptoms of physical pain and emotional distress. Although these symptoms are real, our culture is often dismissive of or downright hostile about them. "Female trouble" is viewed as a disease, rather than a series of natural biological rhythms.

The Turtle Island Project in Arizona offers seminars based on Native American philosophies. Mona Polacca, a Native American educator and facilitator from the Hopi/Havasu tribes, says that being a woman in her tradition is viewed in relation to the natural cycles of the moon: It is continually waxing and waning, a guiding point and a symbol of the natural rhythms of womanhood.

In a 1991 article for *Shape* magazine, Joyce C. Mills, Ph.D., a licensed marriage, family, and child support counselor and hypnotherapist, quoted Polacca and commented, "The changing of our moods lets us know that something important is happening—something to be honored. We don't talk about the moon's changes from half to full as being sick. We don't talk about a tree being defective when it loses its leaves. It is just change, pure and simple." Mills suggested that instead of calling the condition "premenstrual syndrome, PMS, we refer to it as PMA—premenstrual awareness."

The heightened feelings women may have during the menstrual cycle can provide valid insight, too often suppressed and excused by saying "it's that time of the month." "As women, we are in possession of a special pathway to growth and change," Mills said. "Once we choose to put aside the notion that we are

186

saddled with a defect of physiology, we can have compassion for ourselves. What we feel is natural; we shouldn't be too hard on ourselves, nor should we use it as an excuse for not dealing with our lives."

HEART INTELLIGENCE

Your "heart" breaks, it aches, it swells, it grows fond of, it sings, it warms, it yearns. We give it, we take it to, things come from it. Other cultures in addition to ours give power to the heart, as in heart chakra, energy centers, and a similar use of the language to indicate that the heart has a mind of its own. Interesting new research is being done to see if the heart really does have its own intelligence, as opposed to the belief that all mental and emotional activity derives from the brain alone.

187

You may have heard stories that people who have received heart transplants suddenly experience feelings, urges, or appetites previously foreign to them. Scientific investigation exploring the heart in a new way has just begun, but we do know that relaxation makes the heart feel good, figuratively and literally. In heart disease treatment, "Most risk reduction programs acknowledge the importance of stress management and psychological factors," says the Institute for HeartMath. "However, their focus is primarily on diet and exercise, and the interventions rarely include effective stress-management strategies.

"That psychological factors are critical determinants of disease outcome has been clearly demonstrated in a number of recent studies. Anger, anxiety, worry, depression, and emotional reactivity have now all been linked to negative health outcomes."

Still, "even though many physicians recognize that their patients are suffering high levels of personal or job-related stress, they often feel powerless to help them manage and reduce this stress."

Doc Lew Childre, a stress researcher, consultant, and author with Howard Martin and Donna Beech of *The HeartMath Solution,* has developed a program that he believes will foster the communication between heart and head, and provide techniques that can develop heart intelligence to counter stress in the real world.

Some HeartMath Philosophy

According to the Institute of HeartMath, "Heart intelligence can be defined as the intelligent flow of insight that arises once the mind and emotions are balanced and coherent. Appreciation, caring, and compassion are examples of core 'frequencies' within the bandwidth of heart intelligence. Each time you generate one of these frequencies, or positive emotions, your psychology shifts into a more efficient mode.

"As you retrain your emotional and mental reactions and increase your coherence, you will re-create your life. You will reach a place where you no longer have to keep 'working things out,' but realize they are worked out.

"Any time one person makes an effort to contact a deeper part of himself or herself, balance his or her emotions, and deflect the stress momentum, others benefit. As more individuals learn to maintain their poise and balance and refrain from adding to the incoherence around them, they help to counterbalance the frequency of stress."

EMOTIONAL HEALING

Even if you've started exercising, making wise food choices, and giving yourself time out for relaxation, there's often a painful emotional and spiritual history that takes time to become aware of and to resolve. Substance abuse programs such as Alcoholics Anonymous use prayer and meditation, faith in a Higher Power, and honest introspection as tools for living well again.

Deepak Chopra says that by using meditation and focusing techniques, you can clear emotional toxicity. "Begin by taking responsibility for stressors; witness them, define them, locate them in your body, release them, share them, and celebrate them."

The Chopra Center's "Shadow Process" program is about exploring those aspects of ourselves that are "hidden in shadow." "Recognizing that we all have [a] human dark side" is the first step in reaching toward the potential of your higher self. "Most of us want to embrace wholeness, but when you least expect it, too often the dark side will arise to try to wrest control of your life. Accepting both the dark and bright sides, acknowledging the world as holographic, and developing an awareness that we all share these qualities can help you make peace with yourself," says Jude Hedlund, communications manager for The Chopra Center.

Secret shame creates chronic stress. Hedlund describes the experience at this seminar: "While you're on the phone and a child is tugging at you for attention, if you don't respond right away, he will cry louder, tug harder, and become more and more difficult to deal with. If you face him, hug him, acknowledge him, he will quiet down and ease his grip."

189

Spa, hospital, community center, church, temple, synagogue, and wellness clinic programs are making the emotional healing paradigm easier for people to access. Start by taking responsibility for your actions and acknowledging your humanity. Relieve yourself of the burden of shame or embarrassment and recognize that you are different from what you like to think you are. Working with yourself to achieve better control and perspective will lighten your load.

WORK AND STRESS

190

The American Institute of Stress collected surveys and research over the last twenty years that offer disturbing statistics.

- Forty-three percent of all adults suffer adverse health effects due to stress.
- Seventy-five to 90 percent of all visits to primary-care physicians are for stress-related complaints or disorders.
- Research shows a stress connection to many diseases, psychological disorders, and suicide.
- An estimated one million employees are absent on an average workday because of stress-related problems.
- A three-year study by a large corporation showed that 60 percent of employee absences were due to psychological problems such as stress.
- Nearly half of all American workers suffer from symptoms of burnout.
- Forty percent of employee turnover is due to job stress.

- Workplace violence is rampant. Homicide is the second leading cause of fatal occupational injury.

The World Health Organization described job stress as a worldwide epidemic. A 1992 United Nations report called job stress "the twentieth-century disease." In 1973, almost 40 percent of workers reported being "extremely satisfied" with their jobs. Today, fewer than 25 percent fall into that category.

There was a time in this country when it was the goal to get a "good"—i.e., stable—job where you'd stay until you retired, collect your pension and your gold watch, then putter around the house or travel around the world. The transition from goods to services, the rise of computer technology, and the interconnectedness of the world's economies have changed the plan. Most workers switch jobs frequently, and even change careers several times. And while job-hopping may have certain benefits, beginning a new job is something most of us find stressful.

Unrelenting stress and tension lead to burnout—a combination of emotional exhaustion and physical fatigue. A study in *Behavioral Medicine* reported a link between burnout and work performance, job satisfaction, withdrawal behavior, quality of life, psychological well-being, and an increased risk of cardiovascular disease. Samuel Melamed, Ph.D., head of the Behavioral Medicine Unit at the Occupational Health and Rehabilitation Institute in Raanana, Israel, led the team of researchers.

One of the biggest blessings in life is to be able to work at something you like, but even if you're so lucky, they don't call it "going to fun," they call it "going to work." Whatever you do to earn a living, you must make time to remember your body and spirit while you're minding the store.

191

TIME MANAGEMENT

Phones, faxes, pagers, E-mail—we've switched from a chicken in every pot to a cell phone in every car. You can't run and you can't hide. But you can schedule your time to include time-outs. A little organization can go a long way, if you stick to the program. You have to put in your time at work, you have to have your teeth cleaned, you have to have your car serviced, but you have to pay attention to your mind, body, and spirit, as well.

Prioritize

It is imperative that you plan for change. Making a long-term business plan and then breaking it down into short-term steps will help you focus on the job at hand. Reassessing it regularly will save time in the long run, because you will be able to correct the course for the unforeseen factors that inevitably arise. With each short-term assessment, prioritize again. Then abandon unrealistic expectations. Build in enough time to deal with each task in your plan—you can't accomplish anything if you are not realistic about what it takes to follow through.

You can prioritize each day if you are ready to organize the mountain of mail, memos, E-mail, and phone messages. Keep more than one in-basket or file by the time or date you need to deal with each item.

Better yet, "handle it only once," say Yvonne Middleton and Mary Gendron, who head up a team of account executives in their busy New York public relations firm, Middleton & Gendron. "If you deal with a piece of paper as it comes up, you avoid feeling overwhelmed by unfinished business," says Middleton. "Most of the letters people receive entail simple tasks that can be easily taken care of on the spot."

Gendron advises handling E-mail the same way. "Too often, I used to go through my E-mails—and it can really stack up if I've been out of the office—while I was thinking of something else, or doing two things at once," she says. "When I would glance through to check the messages and store them to look at again later, I'd just have to go through it all again." It may take a little effort, but "if you just focus on the issues at hand, and concentrate to make a decision, you save much more time in the long run."

Take a Break

193

Corporations are recognizing that healthy, happy, relaxed employees are more productive, have less absenteeism, and report more job satisfaction. It is no longer surprising to see chair massage therapists come in to corporate offices weekly to give back and shoulder massages to members of the staff. Some companies have installed fitness facilities or sponsor memberships to local gyms. Insurance companies are beginning to include complementary and alternative medicines (CAMs) such as massage and acupuncture in the treatments they cover. Humorous presentations are often part of a convention agenda, and corporations are turning to spas for meetings and retreats.

Morgan Urquhart Edwinson, M.A., is the wellness services manager for Consensus Health Corporation. The company has developed multispecialty networks of complementary and alternative medicine health plans that include stress management and biofeedback. Edwinson says, "Health plans are being pushed into working with CAMs and wellness services by market forces.

Health plans compete for members and their premium dollars, and they want those dollars to come from the healthiest populations possible."

Workday Stress Relievers

Schedule stress busters throughout the day. Set a kitchen timer, alarm clock, pager, or watch beeper to remind you when to take short stress breaks during which you can:

- wander outside for a brisk walk or slow stroll
- meditate for ten minutes by focusing your complete attention on an object, or on your breath
- call a friend to chitchat about something nonwork related
- do some stretching exercises
- eat a healthy snack

Take a break from typing every hour at the very least. Use this time to massage your hands. Use your thumbs to massage each opposite hand in small firm circles for ten seconds. Begin at the base of your palm, and methodically work your way up to the base of each finger. Use the thumb and forefinger to give the space between each finger a firm pinch, and to pinch your way up to each fingertip. Finish by interlacing your fingers and extending your arms while turning the heels of your hand outward for five seconds.

Source: Adapted from *Tips for Your Home Office* by Meredith Gould (Storey Books, 1998). Used with permission.

Practice "Safe Stress" at Work

Here are a couple tips for reducing stress in the workplace from The Stress Doctor, Mark Gorkin, L.I.C.S.W. He is called the on-line psychohumorist for the AOL resource "Online Psych," and writes a cyber-newsletter, *Humor from the Edge*. Gorkin says you can learn to master your stressors by being proactive when it comes to things that can drive you crazy.

Telephone Tremors: Do you start shaking when the phone rings? Or, can't set limits on yourself and others? Are you ready to rewrite the old AT&T television commercial—one more abrasive caller or intrusive telemarketer and you will "reach out and crush someone!" Take control of the telephone. Don't allow others to keep interrupting you. If you think Alexander Graham Bell was "the father of stress," you probably have not cut the cord with your mother. Enough already!

Type-A Trap: Are you reluctant to delegate work because no one can do it as efficiently or perfectly as you? Be careful. You may be setting up a self-fulfilling prophecy. People may start agreeing: "You're right. No one can do it quite like you. Please, do it yourself!" You know, of course, who's the real type A . . . the person who won't settle for anything less than being a type A+.

195

Having done research on health education, psychology and behavioral health, kinesiology, and holistic medicine, Edwinson thinks the trend toward CAMs goes well beyond market forces. "I think everyone functioning in modern society is aware and has experienced the impact that chronic stress can have on the mind, body, and soul," she says. "Although this is a long path, once people get a taste of what it's like to feel good, and feel centered, they naturally want more. Stress-reduction tools like biofeedback, mindfulness-based stress reduction, and guided imagery offer people a glimpse of seeing differently and feeling better fairly quickly," she adds.

Edwinson's company is working with the Jon Kabat-Zinn Center for Mindfulness at the University of Massachusetts, and with Duke University, to develop standards for stress-management providers. Check with your employer and insurance provider to see if you can avail yourself of coverage for CAMs as health services. If you have the freedom to choose your health-care provider, seek one that offers complementary and alternative therapies for preventive-maintenance wellness along with stress-management adjuncts to allopathic treatment.

196

PSYCHOTHERAPY

When relaxation techniques alone are not enough to break the cycle of habitual responses to stressors, you may need professional help. Psychotherapy is useful for those people who need guidance in examining past reactions to stressors, and who need to learn new perspectives and methods of handling them.

Stan Charnofsky, Ed.D., president of the Association for Humanistic Psychology and professor at California State University at Northridge, has learned to relax using deep breathing, exercise, diversion, and "letting it out." "I talk to a colleague, my daughter, my brother, or a close friend when I feel stressed," he says.

Humanistic psychology "is a democratic approach in which the connection between doctor and client is a two-way street . . . a therapeutic relationship that allows people to try out new ways of being," Charnofsky says. It looks at the human being holistically and considers our conditioned responses as having the potential to be changed for the better. This approach superseded the famous dog studies of Ivan Pavlov, called "the conditioned reflex," and the rat boxes of B. F. Skinner that demonstrated stimulus–response conditioning. Our ability to "self-actualize," coined by Abraham Maslow, became the watchword of humanistic psychology. By trying to figure out why we react—or overreact—to stressors, and by learning to manage them, we are attempting to make the best of ourselves.

197

The mind is strongly influenced by forces such as society and the unconscious; some therapeutic techniques can facilitate personal skills and enhance quality of life. A "search for meaning" is a primary human motivation, an awareness that you are not merely a product of biology, heredity, and environment, but that you have a choice about how to react to inner conditions and outer circumstances. This is a key philosophy in stress management: You are responsible for managing your stress. You have the ability to desensitize yourself to the stress-reacting behavior patterns formed in childhood.

Let It Out

"Letting it out," "talking it over," "role-playing," "behavior mod-ification," and "changing perspective" are some of the therapeutic approaches of humanistic psychology that have formed the basis for current stress-management and relaxation practices. Albert Ellis had a model of behavior that A might be true, and B might be true, but we skip C and go right to D, which isn't true, but we react—stress out—as if it is. Charnofsky demonstrates this way:

A) I broke my sister's radio.

B) She got upset, and I did do it.

C) I didn't mean to and I'm sorry (the ameliorating message).

D) I am an awful person.

If you can manage to keep C in your thought processes, even if you are disturbed and stressed at the moment, you can rationally dismiss it and ease away the stressful reaction with relaxation. If you dwell on D, psychotherapy may be a way to break free from some locked-in, self-defeating stress reactions.

Bodywork, concentration, and meditation are techniques explored in humanistic psychology that are commonly suggested for anxiety and stress management. Often, some of the therapy techniques discussed in chapter 4 are used as adjuncts to psychotherapy or counseling. Another psychotherapeutic skill that helps allay stress is learning to be "in the moment." This mindfulness is a concept that forms the basis for many stress-reduction techniques.

Just Don't Do It

When negative reactions and thoughts keep cropping up and you don't have the opportunity for visualization, guided imagery, or deep breathing, give yourself a cue that will remind you this is something you don't want to do to yourself anymore. A good technique for thought-stopping: Put a rubber band around your wrist and snap it when you feel the old stuff oozing up. Pretty soon you'll just be able to hear "snap" in your mind, and you'll have tamed some of the demons.

SPIRITUALITY

Faith sustains many people in times of trouble. In addition to being a source of personal value and purpose, religion serves as the town square and medicine man of old for those who attend today. If organized religion is not your thing, you can pray at the altar of Nature; the power of the vast ocean, towering mountain range, or endless desert can elicit powerful feelings and help you to see things more clearly. You can pray to Jesus or Yahweh, Buddha or Allah, a god or goddess. Use your own Almighty Power or the power of the universe—in any case, this "earnest plea" of prayer can help you be all you want to be.

If you believe, you don't need anyone to tell you the value of spirituality. If you don't, be aware that many stress experts are including a spiritual dimension as demonstrably important in freeing the body from dis-ease. In *Timeless Healing: The Power and Biology of Belief*, Herbert Benson and Marg Stark call it "The Faith

Factor," "remembered wellness plus the elicitation of the relaxation response." In Benson's studies, people who felt a spiritual presence—God—demonstrated the greatest medical benefits from prayer and relaxation. Malarkey refers to it in his work, as does almost every healing modality of ancient culture.

On Gratitude

Being thankful for the things we have, as opposed to concentrating on the problems, can give us an instant lift. Gratitude and giving to others have become mantras, thanks to TV hosts like Oprah Winfrey and Rosie O'Donnell. One of the authors that Oprah promoted, Sarah Ban Breathnach, author of *Simple Abundance,* advocated an easy technique that was adopted by thousands: gratitude journaling.

"Both abundance and lack exist simultaneously in our lives, as parallel realities. It is always our conscious choice which secret garden we will tend . . . when we choose not to focus on what is missing from our lives but are grateful for the abundance that's present—love, health, family, friends, work, the joys of nature and personal pursuits that bring us pleasure—the wasteland of illusion falls away, and we experience Heaven on Earth."

Volunteerism

Whether for God or for humankind, doing for others helps you feel better. The Institute for Touch Research in Miami showed that people who gave massages benefited as much as those they gave it to. Research has shown that those who get out and about are better off than loners. I don't know if any studies have been done on the physiological benefits of volunteering, but I would bet the endorphins run rampant.

Opportunities to help others don't have to be formal commitments. You can look out for the elderly person who lives alone down the block, or pitch in for an occasional fund-raiser. If you have time, you can volunteer in a capacity that uses the valuable skills you've learned by living life, and in an area of interest to you so that you can keep growing and enjoying.

The newspapers, religious newsletters, radio and television stations, and the World Wide Web are all sources to learn about volunteer opportunities. *U.S.A. Weekend* sponsors a Make A Difference Day, a national day of volunteering held annually on the fourth Saturday of October throughout the United States. If you try www.idealist.org, you can view a list of hundreds of interests that need your help, organized by state. Check for more resources in the back of this book.

There are organizations for children and the elderly, for the healthy and sick, from museums to film preservation. If you have the time, preserve your sense of humanity and spirituality by giving of yourself. It may make you healthier, and it surely will give you perspective for stress management.

201

Putting It All Together

Some days, the things you usually do to cope with stress are enough. Then, there are times you could go down the list of all the theories and practices in this book and they wouldn't be enough to keep you calm.

ONE WOMAN'S STORY

Barbara Saltzman found herself face-to-face with a parent's worst fear. She was an editor at the *Los Angeles Times* when her son, David, was diagnosed with Hodgkin's disease. While he was undergoing radiation treatments, the Yale honors student worked on a children's book about a court jester who discovers that the world has lost its sense of humor and who teaches people to find laughter again. David had an optimistic outlook and a deep sense of spirituality, and in the hospital he often shared his story to hearten the sick children. Sadly, he died eleven days before his twenty-third birthday in 1990. He had asked his parents to have his life-affirming book published and to see that kids who needed the book would have it.

Struggling to cope with her grief, Saltzman sought out publishers, but they all would have compromised David's vision. When she could, she spent time in the garden she and David had planted, trying to think things through. Ultimately, Saltzman and her husband, Joe, took out a loan against their home to accomplish their mission: Not only did Saltzman publish and market the book herself, it reached the *New York Times* best-seller list. She quit her job to oversee *The Jester Has Lost His Jingle*, and established the Jester & Pharley Pfund, a nonprofit organization.

"Sharing David's book with children in schools and hospitals is particularly rewarding," Saltzman says. "Written notes and responses from parents, teachers, and children telling me how much the book means to them and how much David himself inspires them means everything to us." She has less time for her "remembering gardening" but still plants flowers in "David's corner." "The grief is continual," she says, "but the responses are continual healing, too. That his message of laughter, hope, joy, and never giving up has made a difference in the lives of so many others, makes us grateful for him and the gift he was to the world."

After her loss, Saltzman had to call upon all her resources to keep going. She was able to maintain a sense of spirituality and gratitude because David had. Gardening became more than a hobby; it became a ritual, a sanctuary. She is perpetually inspired by the stories of people she meets in hospitals and schools, even as she serves as an inspiration to others. "We can all learn from each other and take positive action to get through life."

SYNTHESIZE
STRESS MANAGEMENT

Like Saltzman, you can use the resources of mindfulness, spirituality, support groups, assertiveness, meditation, nature, hobbies, ritual, sanctuary, gratitude, optimism, and volunteering. The information presented here can keep you going when the negative effects of stress might otherwise immobilize you. The main thing is to find some practice, activity, or inspiration that will keep you putting one foot in front of the other while you regain perspective. You can take control of stress relief. Now, relax.

205

RESOURCES

ORGANIZATIONS

Academy for Guided Imagery
P.O. Box 2070
Mill Valley, CA 94942
1-800-726-2070
fax (415) 389-9342
www.healthy.net/agi

American Academy of Child
& Adolescent Psychiatry
3615 Wisconsin Ave. NW
Washington, DC 20016
(202) 966-7300
fax (202) 966-2891
www.aacap.org

American Cancer Society
1-800-ACS-2345 (227-2345)
www.cancer.org

American Chronic Pain
Association
P.O. Box 850
Rocklin, CA 95677
(916) 632-0922
fax (916) 632-3208
www.theacpa.org

American Dietetic Association
216 W. Jackson Blvd.
Chicago, IL 60606-6995
(312) 899-0040
1-800-366-1655
www.eatright.org

American Heart Association
National Center
7272 Greenville Ave.
Dallas, TX 75231-4596
1-800-AHA-USA1 (242-8721)
www.americanheart.org

American Heart Association
(Women's Health Info)
1-888-MY-HEART (694-3278)
http://women.americanheart.org

American Institute of Stress
124 Park Ave.
Yonkers, NY 10703
(914) 963-1200
fax (914) 965-6267
www.stress.org

American Massage Therapy
Association
820 Davis St., Ste. 100
Evanston, IL 60201-4444
(847) 864-0123
fax (847) 864-1178
www.amtamassage.org

American Music Therapy
Association
8455 Colesville Rd., Ste. 1000
Silver Spring, MD 20910
(301) 589-3300
fax (301) 589-5175
www.musictherapy.org

American Psychosomatic
Society
6728 Old McLean Village Dr.
McLean, VA 22101-3906
(703) 556-9222
fax (703) 556-8729
www.psychosomatic.org

Association for Applied
Psychophysiology and
Biofeedback (formerly
the Biofeedback Society
of America)
10200 W. 44th Ave., Ste. 304
Wheat Ridge, CO 80033-2840
1-800-477-8892; (303) 422-8436
fax (303) 422-8894
www.aapb.org

Association for Humanistic
Psychology
45 Franklin St., Ste. 315
San Francisco, CA 94102
(415) 864-8850
fax (415) 864-8853
http://ahpweb.org

Bonnie Prudden Pain Erasure
(Myotherapy)
P.O. Box 65240
Tucson, AZ 85728-5240
1-800-221-4634
(520) 529-3979
fax (520) 529-6679
www.bonnieprudden.com

CDC National Prevention
Information Network
A Service of the National
Center for HIV, STD, and
TB Prevention
1-800-458-5231
www.cdcnpin.org

Centers for Disease Control
and Prevention
1600 Clifton Rd.
Atlanta, GA 30333
1-800-311-3435
www.cdc.gov

Day Spa Association
P.O. Box 5232
West New York, NJ 07093
(201) 865-2065
fax (201) 865-3961
www.dayspaassociation.com

Delta Society (Pet Partners)
289 Perimeter Rd. East
Renton, WA 98055-1329
1-800-869-6898
fax (206) 808-7601
www.deltasociety.org

ERIC Digest
Clearinghouse on
Handicapped and Gifted
Children
Reston, Virginia
1-800-LET-ERIC (538-3742)
www.ed.gov/databases/ERIC_
Digests/ed295396.html

Food Guide Pyramid Booklet
U.S. Department of
Agriculture/Human
Nutrition Information
Service
August 1992, Leaflet No. 572
Superintendent of Documents
Consumer Information Center
Department 159-Y
Pueblo, CO 81009
www.usda.gov

Hakomi Institute
P.O. Box 1873
Boulder, CO 80301-1026
1-888-421-6699
(303) 499-6699
www.hakomi.com

Hellerwork International, LLC
406 Berry St.
Mount Shasta, CA 96067
1-800-392-3900; (530) 926-2500
fax (530) 926-6839
www.hellerwork.com

The Humor Project
480 Broadway, Ste. 210
Saratoga Springs, NY 12866-2288
(518) 587-8770
fax (518) 587-8771
www.humorproject.com

IDEA
6190 Cornerstone Ct. East,
Ste. 204
San Diego, CA 92121-3773
1-800-999-4332
(858) 535-8979
fax (858) 535-8234
www.ideafit.com

Institute of HeartMath
14700 W. Park Ave.
Boulder Creek, CA 95006
(831) 338-8700
fax (831) 338-9861
www.heartmath.com

Institute of Thai Massage, USA
P.O. Box 1272
Boynton Beach, FL 33425-1272
1-800-882-0903
(561) 582-5349
www.thaimassage.org

International Spa Association
546 E. Main St.
Lexington, KY 40508
1-888-651-ISPA (651-4772)
fax (606) 226-4445
www.globalspaguide.com

National Association of Anorexia Nervosa and Associated Disorders (ANAD)
P.O. Box 7
Highland Park, IL 60035
(847) 831-3438
fax (847) 433-4632
www.anad.org

209

National Center for
Complementary and
Alternative Medicine
(NCCAM)
P.O. Box 8218
Silver Spring, MD 20907-8218
1-888-644-6226
fax (301) 495-4957
http://nccam.nih.gov/
http://altmed.od.nih.gov

National Council on
Alcoholism and Drug
Dependence (NCADD)
12 W. 21st St.
New York, NY 10010
1-800-NCA-CALL (622-2255)
fax (212) 645-1690
www.ncadd.org

The National Heart, Lung,
and Blood Institute
Information Center
P.O. Box 30105
Bethesda, MD 20824-0105
(301) 592-8573
fax (301) 592-8563
www.NHLBI.nih.gov

National Institute of
Ayurvedic Medicine
584 Milltown Rd.
Brewster, NY 10509
1-888-246-NIAM (246-6426)
fax (914) 278-8215
www.niam.com

National Institutes of Health
(NIH)
Bethesda, MD 20892
(301) 496-4000
www.nih.gov

National Library of Medicine
8600 Rockville Pike
Bethesda, MD 20894
1-888-346-3656
(301) 594-5983
http://igm.nlm.nih.gov

National Mental Health
Association
1021 Prince St.
Alexandria, VA 22314-2971
1-800-969-NMHA
(703) 684-7722
TTY 1-800-433-5959
fax (703) 684-5968
www.nmha.org

National Self-Help
Clearinghouse
25 W. 43rd St., Room 620
New York, NY 10036
(212) 840-1259
www.selfhelpweb.org

National Sleep Foundation
1522 K St. NW, Ste. 500
Washington, DC 20005
fax (202) 347-3472
www.sleepfoundation.org

Process Acupressure
128 D Oxford Rd.
Moseley, Birmingham
United Kingdom B13 9SH
0121 449 5234

Retreats International
P.O. Box 1067
Notre Dame, IN 46556
1-800-556-4532
(219) 631-5320
fax (219) 631-4546
www.nd.edu/~retreats/

The Turtle Island Project
5624 W. Edgemont Ave.
Phoenix, AZ 85035
(908) 753-9489
www.drjoycemills.com

Upledger Institute
(massage/bodywork therapies)
11211 Prosperity Farms Rd.,
Ste. D-223
Palm Beach Gardens, FL
33410-3487
1-800-233-5880; (561) 622-4334
fax (561) 622-4771
www.upledger.com

U.S. Department of Health
and Human Services
(202) 690-6343
www.healthfinder.gov

Waterbalancing
inAqua Institut
Auweg 1
D-93333 Neustadt
Germany
011 49-9445-970280
fax 011 49-9445-970281

Worldwide Aquatic
Bodywork Association
(Watsu)
P.O. Box 889
Middletown, CA 95461
(707) 987-3801
fax (707) 987-9638
www.waba.edu

Zero Balancing Association
P.O. Box 1727
Capitola, CA 95010
(831) 476-0665
fax (831) 475-0525
www.zerobalancing.com

Counseling Information and Referrals

American Psychiatric Association
Public Affairs, Ste. 501
1400 K St. NW
Washington, DC 20005
(202) 682-6220
fax (202) 682-6850
APA fast FAX on Demand
1-888-357-7924
www.psych.org

American Psychological Association
750 First St. NE
Washington, DC 20002-4242
(202) 336-5800
www.apa.org
http://helping.apa.org

Anxiety Disorders Association of America
11900 Parklawn Dr., Ste. 100
Rockville, MD 20852-2624
(301) 231-9350
fax (301) 231-7392
www.adaa.org

Canadian Mental Health Association
2160 Yonge St., 3rd floor
Toronto, Ontario M4S 2Z3
(416) 484-7750
fax (416) 484-4617

David Rapkin / UCLA Mind-Body Medicine Group
Private Practice of Clinical and Health Psychology and Organizational Development
3130 Wilshire Blvd., Ste. 550
Santa Monica, CA 90403
(310) 828-7395
fax (310) 998-5527

Yoga

**The Expanding Light
at Ananda**
14618 Tyler Foote Rd.
Nevada City, CA 95959
1-800-346-5350
fax (530) 478-7518
www.expandinglight.com

**Kripalu Center for Yoga
& Health**
P.O. Box 793
West St., Rte. 183
Lenox, MA 01240-0793
1-800-741-7353
(413) 448-3400
fax (413) 448-3384
www.kripalu.org

New Age Health Spa
Route 55
Neversink, NY 12765
1-800-NU-AGE-4-U
   (682-4348)
(914) 985-7600
fax (914) 985-2467
www.newagehealthspa.com

213

RELAXATION PRODUCTS

Alpha-Stim
Electromedical Products
  International, Inc.
2201 Garrett Morris Pkwy.
Mineral Wells, TX 76067-9484
1-800-FOR-PAIN (367-7246)
(940) 328-0788
fax (940) 328-0888
www.alpha-stim.com

**ElixirNet World of Health
  Newsletter**
8612 Melrose Ave.
Los Angeles, CA 90069
(310) 657-9300
www.elixirnet.com

The Humor Potential
50 Court St.
Plymouth, MA 02360
1-800-99-TADAH (998-2324)
(508) 746-3998
fax (508) 746-3398
www.stressed.com

Imaginazium
15332 Antioch St., PMB 524
Pacific Palisades, CA 90272
1-800-800-7008
fax (310) 230-0909
www.imaginazium.com
*Yoga Kit for Kids, Empowerment
  Pack for Kids*

**Meditation Goggles and
  Gadgets**
www.biof/mindgear.html

Smart Spa in a Box
SelfCare Catalog
2000 Powell St., Ste. 1350
Emeryville, CA 94608
1-800-816-1673
fax (510) 595-0322
www.selfcare.com

Suki Productions
www.sukiproductions.com

Aromatherapy and Hydrotherapy

Aromatherapy Associates Ltd.
P.O. Box 14981
London, SW6 2WH
United Kingdom
+44 (0) 207 371 9878
fax +44 (0) 207 371 9894
www.aromatherapyassociates.com

Auroma
1007 W. Webster Ave.
Chicago, IL 60614-3502
1-800-327-2025
(773) 248-1173
fax (773) 248-1174
www.auroma.com

The Good Home Company
"Indulgences" by
  Christine Dimmick
www.ThriveOnline.com/Serenity

Judith Jackson Aromatherapy
102 Greenwich Hills Dr.
Greenwich, CT 06831
1-800-548-9928; (203) 531-4089
fax (203) 531-5087

Kerstin Florian, Inc.
15375 Barranca Pkwy.,
  Ste. A-104
Irvine, CA 92618-2217
1-888-KERSTIN (537-7846)
www.kerstinflorianinc.com

215

WEB SITES

www.AahSpa.com
www.breathing.com
www.DiscoveryHealth.com
www.dreamweavers.org
www.fitnesslink.com
www.heall.com
www.healthfinder.com
www.healthy.net
www.kalani.com
www3.bcity.com/kickstress

www.meditationcenter.com
www.noah.cuny.edu/
  alternative/alternative.html
www.eomega.org
www.onhealth.com
www.orientalmedicine.com
www.Oxygen.com
www.shapeup.org
www.thaimassage.org

Experts on the Web

Sara Ban Breathnach
www.simpleabundance.com

Deepak Chopra
www.chopra.com

Richard A. Feely
www.americanwholehealth.com

**Mark Gorkin, The Stress
    Doctor, Frequent Sighers
    Club**
(on-line support/chat group)
www.stressdoc.com

Carl A. Hammerschlag
www.healingdoc.com

Joseph Heller
www.JosephHeller.com

C. Everett Koop
www.drkoop.com

Joseph Kurian
www.kurian.com

Joyce C. Mills
www.drjoycemills.com

Caroline M. Myss
www.myss.com

Lama Ole Nydahl
www.diamond.way-buddhism.org

**Robert Rickover, Alexander
    Technique**
www.alexandertechnique.com

Selye-Toffler University
http://selye-toffler.org

Bernie Siegel
www.drbernie.com

Kathy Smith
www.kathysmith.com

Lloyd J. Thomas
www.creatingleaders.com

Andrew Weil
www.drweil.com

Labyrinths

www.lessons4living.com/labyrinth.htm
www.sacredwalk.com

Substance Abuse

Al-Anon Family Group: www.al-anon.org
Alcoholics Anonymous: www.alcoholics-anonymous.org

Resources

Volunteer Opportunities

www.coolworks.com

www.heartsandminds.org

www.helping.org

www.idealist.org

www.jesterbook.com

www.makeadifferenceday.com

www.servenet.org

BOOKS

Ban Breathnach, Sarah. *Simple Abundance Journal of Gratitude*. New York: Warner Books, 1996.

Bouton, Eldonna. *Write Away: A Journal Writing Tool Kit*, and *Loose Ends: A Journaling Tool for Tying Up the Incomplete Details of Your Life and Heart*. San Luis Obispo, Calif.: Whole Heart Publications, 1999.

Childre, D., H. Martin, and D. Beech. *The HeartMath Solution*. New York: Harper Collins, 1999.

Chopra, Deepak. *How to Know God: The Soul's Journey into the Mystery of Mysteries*. New York: Harmony Books, 2000.

Domar, Alice. *Healing Mind, Healthy Woman*. New York: Henry Holt and Company, 1997.

———. *Self-Nurture: Learning to Care for Yourself as Effectively as You Care for Everyone Else*. New York: Viking, 2000.

Electric Bread: A Bread Machine Activity Book for Kids. Anchorage, Alaska: Innovative Cooking Enterprises, 1998.

Francina, Suza. *The New Yoga for People Over 50*. Deerfield Beach, Fla.: Health Communications Inc., 1997.

Geddes, Anne. *Journals*. San Rafael, Calif.: Cedco Publishing, 1999.

Gillespie, Larrian. *The Menopause Diet*. Beverly Hills, Calif.: Healthy Life Publications, Inc., 1999.

Guiley, Rosemary Ellen. *Dreamwork for the Soul*. New York: Berkley, 1998.

———. *The Encyclopedia of Dreams*. New York: Berkley, 1995.

Hammerschlag, Carl. *The Dancing Healers*. San Francisco: Harper San Francisco, 1989.

Hammerschlag, Carl, and Howard D. Silverman. *Healing Ceremonies: Creating Personal Rituals for Spiritual, Emotional, Physical and Mental Health*. New York: Perigee, 1997.

217

Jackson, Judith. *The Magic of Well-Being.* New York: Dorling Kindersley, 1997.

Kabat-Zinn, Jon. *Full Catastrophe Living: Using the Wisdom of Your Body and Mind to Face Stress, Pain and Illness.* New York: Dell, 1991.

———. *Wherever You Go, There You Are: Mindfulness Meditation in Everyday Life.* New York: Hyperion, 1994.

Kaye, Gloria. *Is There a Healer in the House?* Gloria Kaye, 1997.

Kurian, Joseph. *Living in Beauty.* San Francisco: EMC Publishing, 2000.

Levine, Andrew, and Valerie J. Levine. *The Bodywork and Massage Sourcebook.* Los Angeles: Lowell House, 1999.

Lewis, Dennis. *The Tao of Natural Breathing.* San Francisco: Mountain Wind Publishing, 1997.

Lusk, Julie. *Desktop Yoga.* New York: Perigee Books, 1988.

Malarkey, William B. *Take Control of Your Aging.* Wooster Book Company, 1999.

Mills, Joyce C. *Reconnecting to the Magic of Life.* Imaginal Press, 1999.

Nydahl, Lama Ole. *Entering the Diamond Way: Tibetan Buddhism Meets the West.* Nevada City, Calif.: Blue Dolphin Publishing, 1985; Revised 1999.

———. *The Way Things Are: A Living Approach to Buddhism for Today's World.* Nevada City, Calif.: Blue Dolphin Publishing, 1996.

Olson, Linda Ann. *New Psalms for New Moms: A Keepsake Journal.* Valley Forge, Penn.: Judson Press, 1999.

Pennebaker, James W. *Opening Up: The Healing Power of Expressing Emotion.* New York: Guilford Press, 1997.

———. *Opening Up: The Power of Confiding in Others.* New York: William Morrow, 1990.

Peeke, Pamela M. *Fight Fat After Forty.* New York: Viking Press, 2000.

Sachs, Melanie. *Ayurvedic Beauty Care: Ageless Techniques to Invoke Natural Beauty.* Twin Lakes, Wis.: Lotus Press, 1994.

Saltzman, David. *The Jester Has Lost His Jingle.* Palos Verdes, Calif.: The Jester Co., 1995.

Siegel, Bernie S. *Prescription for Living.* New York: HarperCollins, 1998.

Smith, F. F. *Inner Bridges: A Guide to Energy Movement and Body Structure.* Atlanta: Humanics New Age, 1986.

Weil, Andrew. *Spontaneous Healing.* New York: Alfred A. Knopf, 1995.

AUDIO/VIDEO

*Breathing as a Metaphor for
Living,* David Lewis
P.O. Box 31376
San Francisco, CA 94131
1-888-313-5050
(415) 282-4896
fax (415) 641-7716
www.authentic-breathing.com

Ellipsis Arts
P.O. Box 305
Roslyn, NY 11576
1-800-788-6670
www.ellipsisarts.com

*The Floppy Sleep Game,
The Sound of Dreams*
Dreamtime Productions
1187 Coast Village Rd.,
PMB 457
Santa Barbara, CA 93108
1-888-992-4200
fax (805) 969-9294

Good Night
Greathall Productions Inc.
P.O. Box 5061
Charlottesville, VA 22905-5061
1-800-477-6234
fax (804) 296-4490
www.greathall.com

Living Arts
P.O. Box 3710
Boulder, CO 80307-3710
1-800-254-8464
fax (800) 582-6872
www.livingarts.com

Relax into Excellence audiotapes
The Furthermore Foundation
2309 Glyndon Ave.
Venice, CA 90291
(818) 342-2424

The Relaxation Company
20 Lumber Road
Roslyn, NY 11576
1-800-788-6670
fax (802) 864-1813
www.therelaxationcompany.com

Sound Healers Association
Spirit Music
P.O. Box 2240
Boulder, CO 80306
1-800-246-9764
(303) 443-6023
www.healingsounds.com

**Steven Halpern's Inner Peace
Music**
P.O. Box 2644
San Anselmo, CA 94979-2644
1-800-909-0707
www.stevenhalpern.com

*Stress Relief: Yoga for Beginners,
P.M. Yoga for Beginners with
Patricia Walden*
Living Arts
P.O. Box 3710
Boulder, CO 80307-3710
1-800-254-8464
fax (800) 582-6872
www.livingarts.com

219

*Timeless Healing: The Power
and Biology of Belief,*
Herbert Benson and
Marg Stark
(New York: Fireside, 1996)

*Walking a Sacred Path:
Rediscovering the Labyrinth
as a Spiritual Tool,*
Lauren Artress
(Riverhead Books, 1996)

Whole Person Press
210 W. Michigan St.
Duluth, MN 55802-1908
1-800-247-6789
(218) 727-0500
fax (218) 727-0505
www.wholeperson.com

Yoga for Round Bodies,
Genia Pauli Haddon
Plus Publications
Box 265-R
Scotland, CT 06564
1-800-793-0666

INDEX

222

225

231

Z